BIRDHOUSES

BIRDHOUSES

20 Unique Woodworking Projects for Houses and Feeders

MARK RAMUZ
AND
FRANK DELICATA

STOREY
BOOKS

A QUARTO BOOK

United States edition first published in 1996 by Storey Communications Inc.
Schoolhouse Road, Pownal, Vermont 05261

*The mission of Storey Publishing is to serve our customers by publishing practical information that
encourages personal independence in harmony with the environment.*

This book was designed and produced by
Quarto Inc.
The Old Brewery
6 Blundell Street
London N7 9BH

Senior editors Heather Magrill, Miranda Stoner
Editors Rebecca Myram, Gwen Rigby
Senior art editor Elizabeth Healey
Illustrators Dave McAllister, Tig Sutton, Neil Ballpit, Rob Shone, Gary Cross
Designers Bev Speight and Nigel Wright
Photographers George Solomonides, Martin Norris
Picture research Jo Carlill
Picture manager Giulia Hetherington
American consultant Bob Flexner
Editorial director Mark Dartford
Art director Moira Clinch
Storey Publishing editor Gwen W. Steege

Typeset in Great Britain by Central Southern Typesetters
Manufactured in Hong Kong by Regent Publishing Services Ltd
Printed in Singapore by Star Standard Industries (Pte) Ltd

10 9 8

Library of Congress Cataloging-in-Publication Data

Ramuz, Mark, 1962-
    Birdhouses : 20 unique woodworking projects for houses and feeders / Mark Ramuz
      p.   cm
    ISBN 0-88266-917-6 (alk. paper)
    1. Birdhouses—Design and construction. 1. Title
    OL676.5 R335   1996
    690'.89—dc20   95-33263
                                                    CIP

CONTENTS

A *bluebird just about to enter this simple but sturdy nest box, which is very easy to construct.*

INTRODUCTION

Watching and feeding birds in a yard is one of the most relaxing and rewarding pastimes I have ever come across. And making birdhouses and feeders should be an equally rewarding experience. To this end, we have created twenty projects, ranging in design and difficulty from simple-to-make, natural-wood feeders to an ornate Gothic castle – for birds with a taste for the unusual! We would like all these designs to serve as inspiration for your own adaptations, as well as being accurate working projects. You may want to change the size, the proportions, and the paint finish – or only the placing of the hole. Remember that there are no hard and fast rules. As long as the structure is strong and offers good protection, the styling is up to you. And keep in mind the purpose of the project you build – is it for nesting, for feeding, or both?

BIRDHOUSE BASICS

Although the design of a nesting box is very much a matter of personal taste, here are some basic guidelines for construction, placement, and maintenance.

- The box should have a sloping roof to allow rain to drain off quickly and not soak into the timber. Always drill several drainage holes in the base of any box you make so that water may escape and not rot the wood, or waterlog the nesting material. Drill holes in the sides and/or back for air circulation. Hinged sides or fronts make boxes easier to clean.

- The basic size of the box may vary, but should always be at least 6in (150mm) deep to stop the young from falling out of the entry hole.

- The entry hole may be placed on the front or side and will vary in size depending upon which birds are likely to take a shine to it. As a general rule, however, it should be no more than 1¼–1½in (30–38mm) in diameter. This is large enough to encourage bluebirds, tree swallows, wrens, chickadees, and titmice, yet small enough to prevent larger predatory birds from invading the nest.

- A slot-sided design, such as the Mission Church (page 64), will attract flycatchers. This type of box should be sited in secluded locations, deep in the fork of a tree or secured in a thick hedge.

- The nesting site should be at least 4½ft (1.4m) to 5½ft (1.7m) off the ground so that you can inspect it regularly. Position the entrance hole away from prevailing winds. Conventional locations include the sides of trees or walls.

A nest box secured high up on a tree trunk.

- Birdhouses may be attached to trees or walls in a number of ways. The simplest method is to attach a stout vertical strip of wood to the back of the nesting box, drill a hole in the protruding top section, and nail through this into the tree trunk or masonry. If the tree is particularly delicate, attach the box with a thick rubber or leather strap, screw the ends to the sides of the house and wrap the strap around the trunk.

- Many of the designs in this book can also be placed in open ground on a stout post. Again, secure placement is the key. The post should be at least a 2 x 2in (50 x 50mm) square section, and the end should be driven into the ground at least 1½ft (450mm), more if the ground is soft. At the top of the post, make sure the birdhouse will not wobble by securing it in on all sides with wedge-shaped strips of wood.

A "terraced" birdhouse, with a number of entrance holes, placed on strong posts.

- Keeping predators away is generally more difficult than protecting the birds from the weather. Metal plates nailed around the entry hole may deter squirrels from enlarging the opening.

- Predators, such as cats, racoons, and snakes, may be a problem near birdhouses. Barriers made from stove pipes or sections of slippery metal can be attached to the posts below the house to prevent these creatures from climbing to the nest. Another possibility is to add an extra ¾in (18mm) thickness of wood to the entrance hole to keep paws from reaching eggs and chicks. To form an interior barrier between the predator and the nest, glue three vertical dowels, ½in (12mm) in diameter and 1½in (38mm) long, directly under the inside of the hole and about ½in (12mm) apart.

A traditional dovecote design.

- Avoid disturbing the nesting site because this can easily agitate the adult birds and may cause them to flee.

This chickadee, perched on a branch, is drinking from a hummingbird feeder. You should remember to feed birds regularly.

- You may also find that the birdhouse becomes taken over by bees, wasps, or other insects. There is little that can be done until the box can be cleared out in spring: it is probably best just to put up another birdhouse nearby. Even without infestation, it is worthwhile taking the nest box down in fall, cleaning out the interior and carrying out any repairs. Clear away old nesting material, food, and any dead chicks. In early spring, pour boiling water over the interior surfaces to kill small parasites that could harm future inhabitants. Give natural woodwork a coat of clear water-based wood preservative, and treat any corroded metalwork with a chemical inhibitor before repainting. Provided that you check the nesting box every spring, the wood and metalwork should last for many years.

FEEDER BASICS

Just as different birdhouses attract varying species; similarly, the size and style of the birdfeeder will determine which birds will feed in your yard. Don't feed birds only in winter – a year-round supply of food may bring in a wider range of species.

Remember to put the food out regularly at the same time every day, if possible. If a bird comes to rely on a particular source of food, but finds one day that it is not there, it could die.

- Birdfeeders, like nesters, should have drainage holes drilled in any large horizontal surface.

- Oil-rich mixtures of sunflower seed, millet, and peanut kernels provide a good protein source. Cracked corn and suet attract many varieties of birds; both cheese and meat are welcomed by insect-eating birds. Almost all kitchen scraps can be used to supplement the grain and seed basics though they may also attract predators and pest bird species. Windfall apples and oats could also provide a welcome food supply.

- As when nesting, birds need protection when feeding. Make sure feeding tables are level and firmly attached. A long pole or post, at least 5ft (1.5m) high, will put the birds out of reach of domestic animals, and an inverted tin can pushed halfway up the pole may deter squirrels from stealing the food supply. A slippery plastic section of drain pipe placed over the pole at the base will also serve the same purpose.

- Feeders need more maintenance than nesting boxes. Make sure that kitchen scraps are not left to rot. Put out only the amount of food that will be consumed in one day. Each spring, clean the feeding surfaces with hot soapy water.

MATERIALS

Wood: Solid wood is the most versatile, renewable building material. Its strength, durability and attractive appearance make it the perfect medium for many of the projects in this book.

Sawed or planed softwood needs regular preservative treatment to prevent cracking and rot. Pressure-treated lumber, for optimum protection, is available, but chemicals are used in this treatment and it should not be used for feeding tables or where a bird will be directly nesting. Reserve chemically treated wood for feeder posts, roofing, or the exterior of nesting boxes. If you can obtain scraps of hardwood, the birdhouse will last even longer.

Manmade boards: Plywood and medium density fiberboard (MDF) are used throughout this book. Both provide an economical sheet material for exterior projects and can be sanded, shaped, and painted. Choose exterior grades of plywood or moisture-resistant MDF, but be sure to coat the edges and faces thoroughly with a waterproofing varnish, paint, or sealer. Otherwise water may penetrate the fibers and delaminate the board.

Metalwork: Galvanized nails and plated or brass screws resist corrosion better than steel and do not stain wood. Lead, as on the roof of the Windy Miller house (page 78), is a useful material for sealing joints in roof sections.

- Any other hardware, such as hinges, should be brass wherever possible.

MARK RAMUZ

A solidly built birdhouse that has a weather vane attached to it for added interest and decoration.

This birdhouse for wrens has a long branch, for perching, just beneath the entrance hole.

Feeders, like
birdhouses, should be
placed out of reach of
predators.

Supplying food all the
year round will attract
a wide range of species.

ABOUT BIRDS

The ultimate reward from the labor of making birdhouses comes
when you watch the birds use them. Listen to the musical song of a
male wren singing from a nearby shrub while his mate builds the nest
cup of soft grasses and other plant fibers. Enjoy their animated behavior as
they take turns feeding their young. Maybe you'll witness the fledglings' first
uncertain flight from the box. You can feel proud because you've made something to
help the birds. Although it takes considerable effort to design and build a birdhouse, it is
worthwhile making a little more effort to attract birds to that house.

Only about 15 percent of bird species use nesting boxes. Since a birdhouse duplicates a cavity
found in dead trees, only cavity-nesting birds will use them. Woodpeckers excavate many of
these natural holes in dead trees or snags and, because the excavation process is an important
part of woodpecker courtship and breeding, they make new cavities each year. Other cavity-
nesting birds, such as titmice, chickadees, bluebirds, and wrens will use the same holes year
after year, although very often the occupants are successive generations. Birdhouses which
have been well designed and constructed can be excellent substitutes for traditional nest sites.

The most important consideration in attracting birds to birdhouses is placing them in the correct location.

Birds require three basic necessities: food, water, and shelter.

The greater the variety of these needs you provide, the more species of birds you'll attract. Consider planting an assortment of trees, evergreens, fruit-bearing bushes and trees, grasses, and flowers in your yard to furnish food and shelter for birds. A local nursery or garden center can help with selections that will grow well in your yard. Then integrate feeders, birdbaths, and nesting boxes into the landscape.

It's a good idea to plant an assortment of trees, bushes, and flowers in your yard to supply food and shelter for different birds.

Different species of birds require different habitats. For example, bluebirds rarely nest in urban or forested areas because they prefer open spaces with scattered trees and low undergrowth. They're drawn to edges of large lawns, meadows, pastures, and golf courses. Bluebird nest boxes should be 3–6ft (1–2m) above the ground and 100 yards (90m) apart. Place them near a tree branch or fence for the young birds' first flight and as a convenient perch from which to hunt insects.

Generally birds of the same species do not like to nest close to each other, so it is not necessary to put up more than two boxes for each species in a small yard. Tree swallows, which will nest 19 yards (17m) apart, are an exception. They will nest in bluebird boxes, although they prefer full sun near water.

Titmice and nuthatches, though common at feeders, are woodland birds which prefer open woods and edges for nesting. Their natural sites are

Starlings on a feeder. Seeds, such as millet and peanut kernels, provide protein for birds and most kitchen scraps can be used to supplement grain and seed.

abandoned woodpecker homes – usually in a wooded area. By placing their next box in a similar habitat in your yard, you'll invite these entertaining birds for more than a free meal at your feeder. Both species will use the same size birdhouse, commonly 4 × 4 × 12in (100 × 100 × 300mm) with a 1¼ (30mm) diameter entry. The base of the birdhouse should be placed 4ft–15ft (1.2–4.5m) high.

Two species of flycatcher use nest boxes – the great-crested flycatcher and the western ash-throated flycatcher. Both will accept the same size box, roughly 6 × 6 × 8in (150 × 150 × 200mm) with a 1¾in (43mm) hole situated on a post or tree 8–20ft (2.4–6m) above the ground.

Northern flickers are the most common woodpecker to use nest boxes, but downy, hairy, golden-fronted, and red-bellied will also nest in them. Place the houses 5–15ft (1.5–4.5m) high in a dead snag in a semi-wooded area or an old orchard. For red-headed woodpeckers attach the box approximately 8–20ft (2.4–6m) high on a utility pole or tall tree. Since woodpeckers excavate new cavities each year, it may encourage the birds if you partly fill the nest box cavity with woodchips for them to remove.

Purple martins are the only cavity nesting species east of the Rocky Mountains dependent upon humans for nest sites. Western birds use old woodpecker holes in trees and cacti, but the eastern birds have adapted to living near people.

Purple martins are colony nesters and return year after year to the same apartment-style birdhouse. Place their house on a pole in an open area – ideally by open water – at least 15ft (4.5m) from overhanging limbs or buildings and 14–20ft (4.2–6m) high. Check to be sure that these birds occur in your area before building a martin house.

House sparrows and starlings nest in any cavity or birdhouse they can fit into. The preferred habitat of house sparrows is close to buildings. These two aggressive birds prey on eggs and nestlings and will build nests on top of other birds' nests. Some of the entry hole dimensions, such as those for wrens, are too small for sparrows. But in some houses, such as those inhabited by bluebirds, you may have to keep removing the sparrow nests until they become discouraged and move elsewhere.

It is simple to identify a house sparrow or starling nest: bluebirds, chickadees, and titmice build neat nests; house sparrow and starling nests are messy piles of grasses, feathers, and trash (though tree swallows use feathers).

There are all sorts of designs to choose from when making birdhouses and bird tables. Some may be ornate, others rustic or classical in style. Or you may decide on something really unusual, like these "flying saucers" on the left.

During the nesting season, many birds can be attracted by offering nesting material. Collect bits of unraveled rope, soft cloth, cotton, wool, and moss, cut short lengths of yarn and save hair from a brush or your dog. Do not use long threads, which may get caught in the toes of both baby and adult birds. It is also best to avoid absorbent cotton, which in addition to tangling in claws and feet, will pack down in the nest, making it difficult for the mother to turn her eggs. Place an assortment of suitable materials in baskets or mesh bags near nest boxes – and wait. The rest is up to mother Nature and the birds.

SUSAN DAY

TOOLS & SAFETY

WORKBENCHES

A strong workbench with a vice is an important asset for all woodworkers. They must be anchored so that you can easily perform processes such as planing and sawing. If space is a problem, an excellent alternative to the permanent bench is a metal-framed, foldable workbench. Although limited as a work-surface, it is ideal for clamping boards (even awkwardly shaped pieces).

GOGGLES
Eyes need as much protection as your ears and lungs. Wear goggles whenever you work with power tools, or even hand tools such as hammers.

HEARING PROTECTORS
High levels of noise can damage the hearing. Even if you only use power tools occasionally, wear hearing protectors to protect your hearing.

A dustmask will protect you against fine dust when cutting, routing, or sanding.

DUSTMASKS AND RESPIRATORS

Safety should always be the prime consideration when in the workshop. Cutting, routing and especially sanding produce very fine particles of wood or dust. Make sure you wear a dustmask whenever fine dust is produced.

A more effective form of protection than the lightweight mask is the full-face respirator. This blows clean air over the face to keep dust away. The plastic visor also gives protection against splinters.

POWER TOOLS

While power tools are not absolutely essential, they do remove a lot of hard work from practical tasks, and they can also help to achieve better finished results.

ELECTRIC DRILL
Electric current operated and rechargeable cordless drills are very useful. Some have variable speed settings, forward or reverse action and can be used with twist drill bits, flat or spade bits, auger bits, or screwdrivers.

ELECTRIC JIGSAW
Electric jigsaws can be used for making straight cuts but are ideal for cutting more complex shapes and openings. They can be fitted with different blades depending on the nature of work or material being used. For these birdhouses and feeders a fine jigsaw blade is ideal.

ROUTER
A router may be useful, but is only recommended for the serious hobbyist. Most routers can be fitted with a variety of bits with the ability to cut a wide range of slots and molding profiles.

FINISHING

Being robust outdoor projects, these birdhouses and feeders need a coating that offers good moisture protection rather than a glossy fine furniture finish.

THE GENERAL STAGES OF FINISHING ARE:
• Fill any defects with an exterior wood filler. Sand the wood or board with a medium-grade sandpaper. Always sand in the direction of the grain if possible.
• Brush off the sanding dust and wipe the wood with a cloth dampened with mineral spirits to degrease and clean the surface.
• Coat with your chosen finish. Two thinned coats are better than one thick coat which tends to drip and dry unevenly.

TIPS:
• Do not overload the brush. Apply with even strokes, working the "wet edge" along the grain.
• Support the birdhouse on spikes made from nails hammered through a scrap offcut of wood and inverted on the bench, but be careful.
• Give vulnerable end grain an extra coating to stop water penetration.

HAND TOOLS

Most of the projects in this book can be made with a basic set of woodworking hand tools.

1 HANDSAW

A handsaw is a good general purpose tool for cutting materials to size.

2 BACKSAW

A backsaw is good for straight, accurate cuts, especially for finer work.

3 COPING SAW

A coping saw is invaluable for making entrance holes, decorative trim and other curved work.

MEASURING & MARKING

4 TAPE MEASURE/STEEL RULE

A good quality tape measure and a steel rule are very useful.

5 TRY SQUARE

A try square is essential for marking and checking right angles.

6 SLIDING BEVEL

A sliding bevel is useful for roof slopes and angled sides.

7 MARKING GAUGE

A simple marking gauge is used to mark parallel lines.

CUTTING & PLANING

8 CRAFT KNIFE

A craft knife can be used to mark w accurately and on thin wood will gi clean, splinter-free cut.

9 BEVEL-EDGED CHISEL

Bevel-edged chisels will be useful fo some projects. The most common si are the ½in (12.5mm) and 1 in (25m chisels.

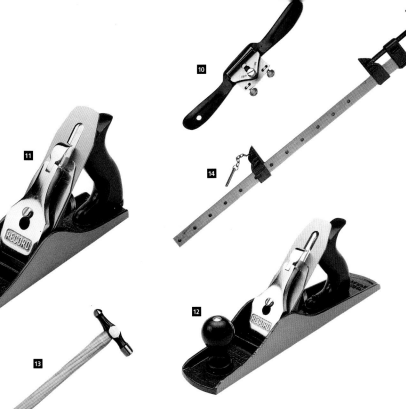

MATERIALS

Wood
Solid softwood and hardwood are
obtainable in standard sizes from your
local lumber yard and sold by the board
or board foot. It is important to note
that the sizes for lumber – (often
referred to as S4S – surformed four
sides) are nominal. For example, if you
buy board with a nominal size of 1 ×
2in (25 × 50mm), the actual size you
will work with is ¾ × 1½in (22 × 45mm),
and so on. This anomaly needs to be
considered when making a cutting plan
for your birdhouse or feeder.

Sheet Boards
Manufactured boards such as veneer
core, plywood, lumber core plywood,
and medium density fiberboard (MDF)
are usually sold in panels 4 × 8ft. A
panel contains 32 square feet.
Manufactured board is priced by the
square foot and by thickness. For
example, plywood ¾in thick will cost
more per square foot than ¼in.
Remember to always buy Exterior Grade
boards; in other words, those glued
with waterproof adhesive.

Adhesives
Yellow glue (polyvinyl acetate) is the
ideal woodworker's glue. When joining
two pieces of wood, ensure that the
surfaces to be bonded are clean, since
glue will not absorb into varnished or
painted surfaces. Apply evenly but
thinly and hold the joint together with
clamps, or in a vise. Wipe off any excess
glue with a damp cloth and leave to set.
   Yellow glue is clean and efficient and
does not stain. Be careful not to spill it
onto surfaces that you wish to color
with a wood stain as it will form a
barrier to stop the stain and may
stand out as an unwanted blemish
in your work.
For these projects, make sure that
you purchase Exterior Grade glue as
this will be waterproof when set.

10 Spokeshave
A spokeshave will help to shape
rounded profiles.

11 Smooth plane
A smooth plane is invaluable for giving
a really good edge, which will be very
helpful when gluing and nailing pieces
of wood.

12 Jack Plane
The heavier jack plane is used for
putting a straight edge on longer
lengths of wood.

13 Hammer
A lightweight hammer up to 4oz
(110gm), is all that is necessary for
brads.

14 Bar and C-Clamps
These will always be helpful for holding
pieces of wood together during the
gluing-up stages.

15 Nail Punch
This can be used to sink countersink
brads below the surface.

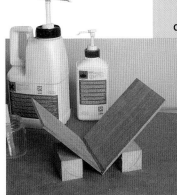

MAKING THE PROJECTS

The following pages contain detailed instructions for making 20 birdhouses and feeders. The designs are arranged roughly in order of complexity, indicated by the number of feathers next to the project title. One feather denotes a simple project while three feathers signify one that is relatively complex.

PERHAPS THE MOST NATURAL OF ALL NEST BOXES IS A HUMBLE PIECE OF HOLLOWED OUT BRANCH. IT PROVIDES A PERFECT HABITAT, AND IS ONE OF THE EASIEST BIRDHOUSES TO MAKE. THIS ONE HAS A PLYWOOD BASE AND MATCHING WOOD ROOF. TO ALLOW THE RAIN TO RUN OFF, ITS PITCHED ROOF IS ATTACHED TO THE

MATERIALS

- 12in (300mm) long section of branch or trunk, 6in (150mm) in diameter
- 6in (150mm) square piece of ⅛in (3mm) plywood
- Brads
- 2in (50mm) flush cabinet hinge and four ¾in (18mm) wood screws
- Two 20in (500mm) long metal straps, ½in (12.5mm) wide
- 2½in (62mm) square piece of ¹⁄₁₆in (2mm) thick metal
- Exterior Grade clear preservative
- Yellow glue

TOOLS

- Panel saw
- Small keyhole saw
- Electric drill
- ½in (12.5mm) wood bit
- Jigsaw
- Hammer
- 1in (25mm) chisel
- Screwdriver
- Paintbrush
- Tape measure

LOG CABIN

TOP WITH A FLUSH METAL HINGE. THE CIRCLE OF METAL AROUND THE HOLE AT THE FRONT PREVENTS PREDATORS FROM ENLARGING THE HOLE, AND A COATING OF WOOD PRESERVATIVE ENSURES THAT YOUR TINY FRIENDS WILL BE ABLE TO NEST HERE YEAR AFTER YEAR.

SUITABILITY

- With an entrance hole of 1¼in (32mm) in diameter, this nesting box is suitable for a wide variety of birds. Place it about 5–11ft (1.5–3.5m) above the ground for bluebirds, titmice, nuthatches, chickadees, and wrens. Other birds, such as downy woodpeckers, hairy woodpeckers, tree swallows, and violet-green swallows, favor a higher location – so put their boxes 6–20ft (2–6m) high. Lower levels make inspection convenient. For all birds, except bluebirds and tree swallows, place this nester near a tree where they will be sure to find it.

1 Cut the bottom of the section of branch or trunk at right angles to the sides with the panel saw.

2 Cut the roof end at an angle of about 30° to allow rain to run off.

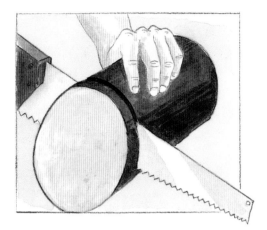

3 Slice off the roof section, making sure it is at least ¾in (18mm) thick and the same depth all the way around. If you need a sawing guide, mark the log at various points, using a tape measure.

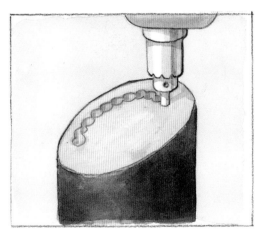

4 Drill closely spaced holes in the center of the log, ¾in (18mm) from the outer surface. Drill to half the depth of the wood. Reverse the log, hold it securely and drill from the other end. Keep the drill vertical so as not to pierce the surface of the log.

Lid

Metal strap

Hollowed out log

Entrance hole

Metal ring nailed to log

Metal strap

Holes for drainage

Plywood base

This exploded diagram shows how the components fit together.

5 Cut around the drilled holes with a keyhole saw.

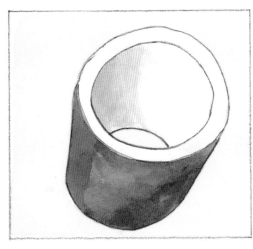

6 Remove the material. For extra smoothness, finish off the hollowing out with a 1in (25mm) chisel.

7 Place the log on a piece of paper and draw around it to make a template for the plywood bottom.

8 Tape the paper to a section of ¼in (6mm) plywood and cut it with the jigsaw.

MADE OF THE HIGHLY FLEXIBLE WOOD, WILLOW, THIS EXOTIC WINGED DESIGN PROVIDES A GOOD SPACIOUS HOME FOR BIRDS.

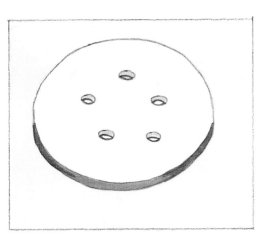

9 Drill five equally spaced holes in the plywood; this allows water to drain.

10 Nail and glue the plywood to the underside of the box.

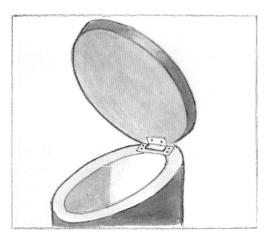

11 Attach the hinge to the roof and the rear, higher, part of the log with the woodscrews.

12 Use a jigsaw to cut a 1½in (38mm) hole at the front, just above the middle of the log.

13 Cut a ⅝in (15mm) wide ring of the ⅟₁₆in (2mm) metal and nail this around the hole with brads.

14 Attach the metal straps tightly toward the top and bottom of the box, nailing with four brads per strap. These loops keep the box intact if the log cracks as it dries out.

When you have finished constructing the log cabin nest box, coat it with a couple of coats of clear exterior preservative and place it at least 5ft (2.4m) above the ground.

GARDENER'S FRIEND

THIS EASY-TO-MAKE FEEDER IS SIMPLY A WEATHERED GARDEN TOOL THAT CONJURES UP IMAGES OF SMALL BIRDS PERCHING ON AN IDLE HANDLE, WAITING FOR A MEAL. THE ADDITION OF A FEEDING TRAY TO AN

MATERIALS

- 14in square (350mm) piece of birch-faced Exterior Grade plywood, ¾in (18mm) thick
- Lengths of 1¼ x 1in (30 x 25mm) oak or other hardwood for edging
- Scraps of 1in (25mm) oak for braces and the central six-sided collar
- 4ft (1220mm) length of 1¼in (30mm) softwood dowel
- 2in (50mm) plated screws
- Yellow glue
- Exterior stain/preservative
- Brads
- Water pot
- Sandpaper

TOOLS

- Jigsaw
- Hand saw
- Molding plane or router
- Hammer
- Try square
- Sliding bevel
- Pair of compasses
- Tape measure and pencil
- Paintbrush
- Electric drill, countersink and bit
- Screwdriver
- Hand plane
- Medium grade sandpaper

GARDENER'S FRIEND

OLD FORK OR SPADE IS A DELIGHTFUL FEATURE FOR A COTTAGE-STYLE GARDEN. THE TRAY IS MADE FROM PLYWOOD AND IS ATTACHED BELOW THE HANDLE. IT HAS A SMALL CUT-OUT FOR A WATER OR SEED POT AND A RAISED EDGE TO PREVENT THE FOOD FALLING OFF ONTO THE GROUND.

SUITABILITY

- This feeder will be especially popular with cardinals, juncos, white-crowned sparrows, song sparrows, and doves, which naturally feed on the ground. However, other birds, such as chickadees, titmice, jays, and nuthatches, will probably also join the feast. Since this feeder, by its very nature, will sit quite close to the ground, it is important that your feathered visitors are protected. Make sure that it is placed in an open, but not too exposed, part of the yard so that the birds will see the approach of potential predators. Also, protect the feeder by adding some type of "predator guard" to the pole.

Handle

Collar

Braces

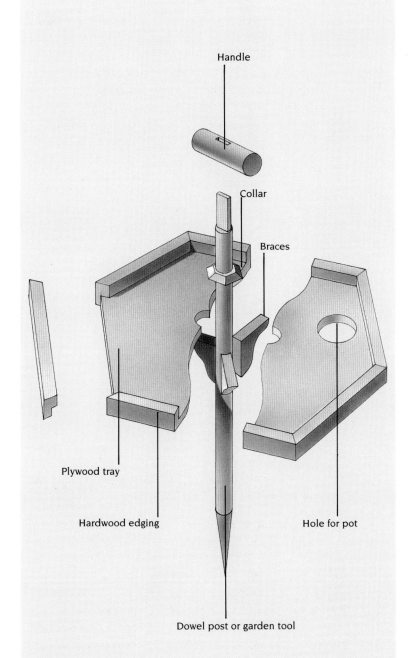

Plywood tray

Hardwood edging

Hole for pot

Dowel post or garden tool

This exploded diagram shows how the components fit together. For the cutting dimensions, see the template on page 110.

METHOD

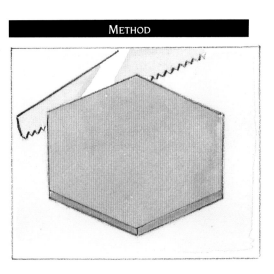

1 Cut the base to size by following the template on page 110 or by using a pair of compasses to draw a circle the required size and marking off the six corners. Connect the points to form a six-sided tray.

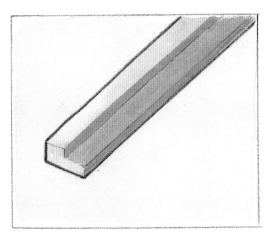

2 Prepare the solid oak edging by routing a rabbet on the underside with a rabbet bit. Alternatively, use a rabbet plane or buy a ready-made molding. Miter the ends to fit around the tray. Use a sliding bevel to obtain the correct angles.

3 Nail and glue the edging to the sides of the tray, flush with the underside.

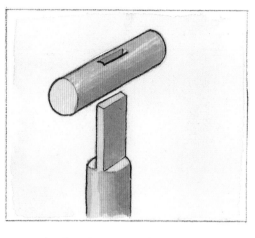

4 Cut the dowel to size and cut pieces out of one end to form a rectangular notch. Shape the bottom edges to match the curve of the dowel crosspiece. Plane the bottom to a point.

7 Plane a flat section on three sides of the upper part of the dowel for the braces and screw these into place.

AN OLD GARDEN FORK WOULD MAKE AN IDEAL GARDENER'S FRIEND. JUST ADD THE TRAY AND STIDCK IT IN THE GROUND ANYWHERE.

5 Cut out the hole for the pot with a jigsaw.

6 Make a posterboard template and cut three supporting braces from the scraps of 1in (25mm) wood. Drill two holes in each brace so that they can be attached to the dowel.

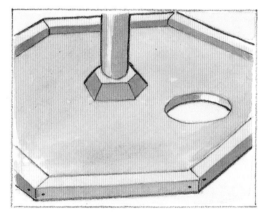

8 Make a small six-sided collar piece of solid oak to match the tray shape. Bevel the top edge with a plane and cut out a hole in the center for the dowel.

9 Slip the collar and tray over the dowel and screw and glue the tray to the top of the braces.

10 Glue and nail the small "handle" to the top of the dowel.

*Before you bury the point
of this feeder in the
ground, paint it with an
Exterior Grade wood
preservative and varnish
or paint it.*

A MORE SOPHISTICATED VERSION OF

THE LOG CABIN (PAGE 20), THE TREE

HOUSE UTILISES A LARGE

TRUNK AND ITS BRANCHES.

IT IS A FEEDER, AND CAN

HAVE AS MANY FEEDING

STATIONS AS IS PRACTICAL,

KEEPING IN MIND THAT A

BRANCH CAN BE WEAKENED

BY TOO MUCH DEEP DRILLING.

CHOOSE A SECTION OF TREE

WHICH IS ATTRACTIVELY

SHAPED AND HAS GOOD

THICK BRANCHES INTO

MATERIALS

● A large branch or trunk with several offshoots
● 20in (508mm) length of ⅜in (9mm) hardwood dowel
● One small glass jar, 1½in (38mm) in diameter, for each feeding station
● Exterior Grade wood preservative

TOOLS

● Electric drill
● 1½in (38mm) flat spade bit
● ⅜in (9mm) spade bit
● Gouge
● Keyhole saw
● Mallet and old chisel

TREE HOUSE

WHICH HOLES CAN BE DRILLED. THIS

BRANCH-STRUCTURED TREE HOUSE

MAKES A FITTING ADDITION TO A

SMALL WALLED YARD AND IT DOES

NOT TAKE UP MUCH SPACE.

SUITABILITY

● Tree branches are the natural feeding place for woodpeckers and nuthatches, so they should be easily attracted to this tree house. Chickadees, titmice, woodpeckers, and nuthatches are happy using a feeder placed between 4–15ft (1.2–4.5m) above the ground. By placing orange halves on nails or spikes, you will also provide a treat for orioles, woodpeckers, and tanagers.

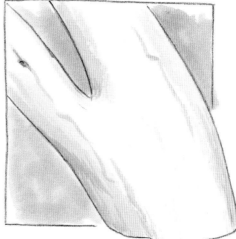

1 If you wish to give the finished feeder a smoother appearance, strip the bark off your chosen piece of wood, using an old chisel and mallet to peel the bark off gently.

2 Prop the branch upright.

3 Cut the base of the branch horizontally with a keyhole saw so that it stands flat. This gives the branch as much stability as possible.

4 Check that the areas where you want to place the feeding pots are not so thin that they will be weakened by drilling.

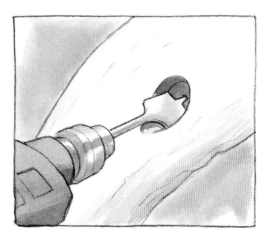

5 Using the 1½in (38mm) spade wood bit, drill each 1½in (38mm) hole. Each pot must fit tightly so that it does not move as the bird feeds.

A SIMPLY CONSTRUCTED NEST BOX, ATTACHED HIGH UP ON A TREE TRUNK.

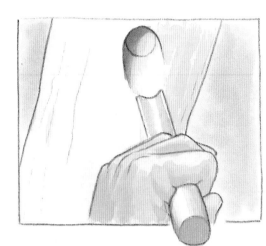

6 Slightly elongate each hole with a gouge or a smaller drill bit to make the jars easier to remove for refilling.

7 Just below each jar, using the ⅜in (9mm) spade bit, drill a hole to accommodate a ⅜in (9mm) dowel, and insert a 2in (50mm) length. This acts as a perch, though some branches may have their own natural twigs which can be trimmed to length.

8 Give the finished feeder a good coating of penetrating wood preservative.

This feeder, made from a tree branch, makes an attractive addition to a small yard, since it does not take up much space.

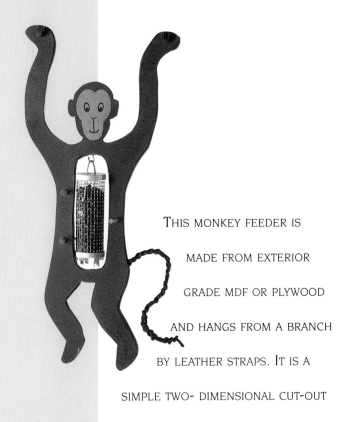

● 12 x 24in (300 x 600mm) piece of 1in (25mm) thick Exterior Grade MDF or plywood
● Pair of thick brown shoe laces
● Approximately 15in (380mm) of hardwood dowel
● Metal hook and 12in (300mm) of thick wire
● Leather straps ½in (12.5mm) wide
● Brown exterior gloss or varnish stain, cream and black paint
● Sandpaper

● Jigsaw or fretsaw
● Electric drill
● ⅜in (9mm) wood drill bit
● Paintbrushes
● Pencil
● Tape measure

THIS MONKEY FEEDER IS MADE FROM EXTERIOR GRADE MDF OR PLYWOOD AND HANGS FROM A BRANCH BY LEATHER STRAPS. IT IS A SIMPLE TWO- DIMENSIONAL CUT-OUT LIKE THE SILENT GARDENER AND

MONKEY NUTS

SQUIRREL NUTKIN (SEE PAGES 38 AND 41). IN THE MIDDLE OF THE CENTRAL BODY SECTION, THERE IS A LONG OPENING IN WHICH TO HANG A FEEDER FULL OF NUTS AND THREE DOWEL PERCHES ARE PLACED CLOSE BY. A SEPARATE TAIL IS ADDED AT THE BACK. SWINGING MONKEY NUTS IS IDEAL FOR ANYONE WHO WANTS TO BRING A TOUCH OF THE JUNGLE TO THE BACKYARD.

The template for this design is shown on page 108.

● This feeder is designed to hold a hanging wire feeder. You can also use a mesh bag of the kind that can be bought in any garden center or pet store. Sunflower and thistle (niger) seeds offered in this way are attractive to many smaller species, including pine siskins, purple finches, and American goldfinches.

During winter try putting suet or peanut butter into a hanging bag. This easy source of energy is a substitute for the insects that birds eat the rest of the year. It will bring especially interesting visitors to your garden, such as nuthatches, blue jays, common flickers, woodpeckers, and mockingbirds.

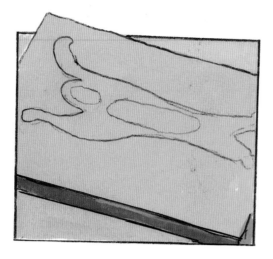

1 Trace out the shape of the monkey, including the central oval, onto the MDF or plywood using the template on page 108.

2 Use a jigsaw or fretsaw to cut out the shape. Make clearance holes at each corner of the central rectangular shape to allow the jigsaw to turn the tight corners when cutting this out.

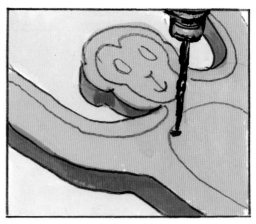

3 Drill two holes for the leather hanging straps, three holes for the dowel perches, a recess for the tail, and a clearance hole to start the cut for the central oval. Cut out the oval.

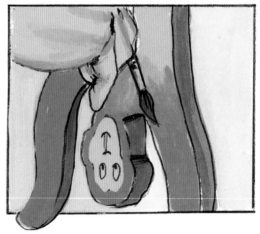

4 Sand any rough edges and paint the MDF with dark brown gloss paint or a varnish stain. Add the face details when the base coat is completely dry.

5 Add the center hook for the food net and the two leather straps, and glue the dowel perches in place. Braid the laces and wire together to form the tail and attach this to the tail recess with a scrap of dowel.

6 Hang the feeder from a branch by the leather straps and hook up a wire feeder or a net of peanuts in the center.

What better way to serve nuts to your feathered friends than with your own swinging monkey, which brings a touch of the jungle to your backyard.

A MINIATURE SHED CAN BE ATTACHED TO THE SHED IN YOUR YARD SO THAT YOU CAN USE A SECURITY PEEPHOLE TO STUDY THE BEHAVIOR OF THE NESTING BIRDS.

MADE OF SOLID WOOD IN A SMALL PITCHED-ROOF DESIGN, THE SHED IS SCORED WITH LINES TO IMITATE THE SHIPLAP PLANK ON A

MATERIALS

● 39in (1m) of 7 x 11in (175 x 25cm) planed pine
● 12 x 12in (300 x 300mm) square piece of ⅛in (3mm) Exterior Grade plywood
● 12in (300mm) x 6in (150mm) piece of roofing felt
● Brads
● ¾in (18mm) nails
● Scraps of wood
● Yellow glue
● Wood preservative
● Black paint
● Door security peephole
● Sandpaper

TOOLS

● Ruler
● Try Square
● Marking gauge
● Backsaw
● 1in (25mm) chisel
● Four 8in (200mm) C- or bar clamps
● 1in (25mm) and ½in (12.5mm) spade bits
● Electric drill
● Plane
● Awl
● Small hammer
● Craft knife
● Metal ruler

MINI SHED

REAL SHED. IT HAS A FELT ROOF SO THAT THE NEST WILL BE KEPT DRY, AND PROVISION IS MADE FOR ATTACHMENT TO A LARGER SHED FOR BIRD-WATCHING.

SUITABILITY

● The really tiny birds – chickadees and house wrens – may go for this birdhouse. Listen for their spirited singing and put this nester 5–15ft (1.5–4.5m) high along the edge of your lawn or, if possible, near woods. By making the entrance hole 1¼in (32mm), you could attract Bewick's wrens, Carolina wrens, titmice, nuthatches, and downy woodpeckers. You can help the birds set up housekeeping by providing them with nesting material. Wrens are especially fond of sticks, so break up small, short twigs and place nearby. A basket filled with 6in (150mm) strips of yarn, bits of moss, cotton, hair, and wool will also be appreciated.

Felt roof held in place with nails

Plywood roof under felt

Entrance hole

Peephole

Walls made of pine

Thin molding used
to make window

Painted door

Plywood base

1 Lay two 12in (300mm) lengths and two 6in (150mm) lengths on the pine, and cut these off with a backsaw.

2 Lay out and cut the slopes for the roof on the two smaller pieces, and trim to the line with a plane.

3 Using a marking gauge, lay rabbets on the long pieces.

4 Cut rabbets 8⅜in (216mm) long x ⅞in (23mm) wide with a backsaw and if necessary trim the joint with a chisel. Make the step in the joint about 1⁄16in (2mm) more than the thickness of the wood.

This exploded diagram shoiws how the components fit together. For the cutting dimensions, see the template on page 111.

5 With a metal ruler as a guide, and using an awl, mark a series of equally spaced parallel lines on the sides of the birdhouse.

6 Using the spade bits and electric drill, make a hole 1in (25mm) in diameter above the front door for the birds to enter and a hole to the side or rear to take your security peephole for viewing the birds.

7 Glue and assemble the four sides with the brads and clamp with the C- or bar clamps. Check with a try square to ensure the sides are at 90° before leaving the glue to set.

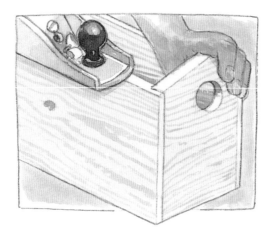

8 Plane the excess on the joint and the long sides to align with the slope for the roof.

9 Sand rough edges and surfaces with medium grade grit sandpaper.

10 Using a backsaw, cut three lengths of plywood: one piece 12 x 6in (300 x 150mm) for the base; and two pieces 12 x 3⅛in (300 x 80mm) for the roof.

11 Glue and nail the plywood pieces to the birdhouse frame, and trim any excess with a plane.

12 Glue and nail the roofing felt to the plywood roof, and trim off any excess with a craft knife.

13 Cut scraps or a piece of thin molding into two pieces 4 x ³⁄₁₆in (100 x 5mm) and three pieces 2 x ³⁄₁₆in (50 x 5mm).

14 Glue all five pieces to the wall, making them into a window shape.

ALTHOUGH THE SHAPE OF THESE BIRDHOUSES IS TRADITIONAL, YOU CAN PERSONALIZE THEM WITH YOUR PAINT FINISH. THESE TWO HAVE A CHEERFUL, SPRINGTIME FEEL.

15 Give the sides and base a coating of wood preservative.

16 Lay out the door.

17 Paint the door and the window in black to highlight their details.

18 Insert the peephole through both the wall of your shed and the birdhouse.

You can place the birdhouse in the fork of a tree, as shown here, or attach it to the wall of your shed, well away from the door, to avoid disturbing the nesting birds as you go in and out. If the birdhouse is attached to a tree, you will not need the peephole in the side wall of the house.

THE INSPIRATION FOR THIS INGENIOUS FEEDER WAS THE DUMB WAITER, FAMILIAR FROM VICTORIAN HALLWAYS AS A PLACE FOR KEEPING LETTERS. IN THIS CASE, HOWEVER, IT IS A SILENT GARDENER HOLDING OUT HIS TRAY OF BIRD FOOD. HE MAKES AN AMUSING FIGURE, PLACED IN A QUIET CORNER OF THE YARD WHERE THE BIRDS WILL

MATERIALS

- 4ft square (1220mm²) section of 1in (25mm) exterior grade MDF
- 1ft square (300mm²) section of ¾in (18mm) exterior grade MDF
- 2in (50mm) plated screws
- Yellow glue
- Exterior paint
- Exterior wood preservative
- Sandpaper

TOOLS

- Jigsaw
- Hand plane
- Electric drill, countersink and wood bit
- Spokeshave
- Try square
- Tape measure and pencil
- Screwdriver
- Paintbrushes

SILENT GARDENER

BE ABLE TO FEED IN PEACE.

BASICALLY, THIS BIRD FEEDER IS A SIMPLE WOOD CUT-OUT, PAINTED TO PROTECT IT FROM THE WEATHER, AND QUICK AND EASY TO MAKE.

SUITABILITY

- This feeder will attract a variety of birds to your garden. Pre-packaged mixes of seeds will serve as a starter, although you would do well to supplement this with extra sunflower seeds, peanut kernels, and millet. Cardinals, finches, chickadees, titmice, jays, and nuthatches love sunflowers served on a tray such as this. You could also try putting out some banana to attract indigo buntings, yellow-breasted chats, jays, and mockingbirds or grapes for bluebirds, robins, and warblers. Apple slices are popular with mockingbirds, woodpeckers, and finches.

1 Trace the gardener's shape along one side of the thicker MDF board from the template on page 109. You could use a projector to blow up a slide image or simply experiment until you have a profile you like.

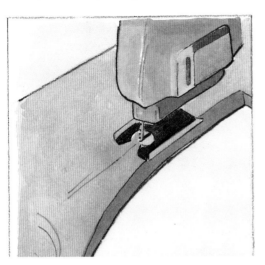

2 Carefully cut around the line with a jigsaw. Work slowly and make several exit cuts into tight corners so that the blade does not become stuck.

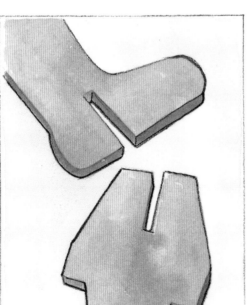

3 Prepare the foot spike in the same way, using the remains of the thicker MDF board. Cut a notch in the bottom of the gardener's boot and the top of the spike. Both must be central and around 6in (150mm) deep. The notches should be made 1in (25mm) wide so that the two pieces will form a strong joint.

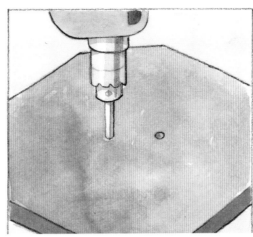

4 Next, make the feeder tray from the thinner MDF. Miter the corners to make a more compact shape. Drill two holes in the center so that the tray can be screwed to the hand of the figure.

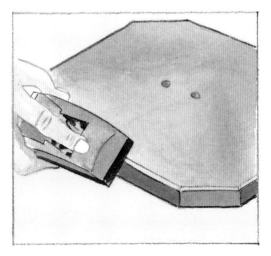

5 Bevel the top edge all the way around with a hand plane or sanding block.

AN ATTRACTIVE AND UNUSUAL HALLOWEEN WITCH, WHICH BIRDS CAN PERCH ON .

6 Use a spokeshave to round both sides of the cut edge of the figure and lightly sand the whole surface.

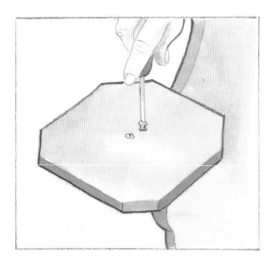

7 Screw and glue the tray to the figure.

8 Paint the MDF with eggshell or gloss exterior colors and treat the foot spike with an exterior wood preservative as well. Stick the spike into the ground and slot the figure in place.

The template for this design is shown on page 109.

Although simple to make, this feeder will be an attractive and amusing addition to any yard.

SQUIRRELS OFTEN TAKE THE FOOD THAT YOU PUT OUT FOR THE BIRDS BEFORE THEY HAVE A CHANCE TO GET TO IT. OUR SQUIRREL NUTKIN IS A VISUAL PUN ON THIS IDEA: HE HOLDS A SIMPLE ROUND TERRACOTTA POT

SQUIRREL NUTKIN

BETWEEN HIS FRONT PAWS, OFFERING FOOD TO THE BIRDS INSTEAD. A SIMPLE TWO-DIMENSIONAL CUT-OUT LIKE THE SILENT GARDENER (SEE PAGE 38), THE SQUIRREL IS MADE FROM EXTERIOR GRADE MDF, CUT WITH A JIGSAW. IT CAN BE ATTACHED TO A TREE, POST OR FENCE.

METHOD

1 Make a line drawing of the squirrel on a piece of paper using the template on page 125. Stick the paper with spray adhesive to the piece·of 1in (25mm) MDF.

2 Clamp the material to your work surface so that part of it is hanging over the edge.

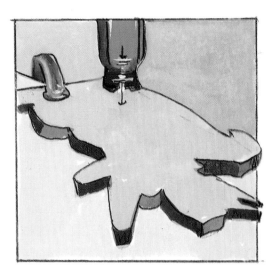

3 Cut around the silhouette line with a jigsaw fitted with a fine blade.

4 File the edges of the MDF to remove any saw marks.

5 Mark the positions of dowel holes and drill with a ⅜in (10mm) twist drill bit.

6 Cut two 4in (100mm) lengths of ⅜in (10mm) dowel for the strapping handles.

7 Drill two ³⁄₁₆in (5mm) diameter holes in the squirrel, 1in (25mm) apart on the lower arm.

8 Cut two strips of wire to a length of 12in (300mm) with a pair of pliers or wire cutters.

9 With the aid of pliers, bend one piece around a can or solid circular object which is the same diameter as the terracotta pot. Twist the ends together and cut off the excess, leaving a tail of about 1⅛in (30mm). Repeat this with the second piece of wire.

10 Lay the two wire rings together and insert the tails into the two ¼in (6mm) holes.

11 Finish by sanding and applying red or brown stain preservative.

12 Pick out any details with paints applied with a fine artist's brush.

13 Insert two ⅜in (10mm) dowels and strap the squirrel to a tree.

This feeder will provide you with hours of entertaining bird watching – especially if the squirrels try to share the food you have put out.
The template is shown on page 125.

THIS OPEN-SIDED

FEEDER HAS A

DISTINCTIVE MOCK CEDAR SHINGLE

ROOF MADE FROM STAGGERED STRIPS

OF SOLID WOOD ON A PLYWOOD

BASE WHICH MAKES A PLEASING

CONTRAST TO THE REST OF THE

WHITE-PAINTED STRUCTURE. THE

SQUARE SUPPORTING POSTS SLOT

MATERIALS

● 4ft square
(1220mm²) of ½in
(12.5mm) Exterior
Grade plywood
● 1 x 1¼in (25 x 30mm)
softwood strips of
wood
● 1¼in square
(30mm²) piece of
softwood strip
● 1 x ¼in (25 x 6mm)
softwood strips for
roof tiles
● 1¼ x ¼in (30 x 6mm)
softwood for trim
● Scraps of ⅜in (9mm)
Exterior Grade
plywood
● Brads
● Yellow glue
● Sandpaper
● Exterior
stain/preservative
● Exterior gloss paint
● Water pot
● Water pot

TOOLS

● Router, rabbet and
decorative bit
● Jigsaw
● Drill, bit
● Hand saw
● Hand plane
● Try square
● Tape measure and
pencil
● Hammer
● Paintbrush

SWISS CHALET

INTO THE RECTANGULAR BASE AND

TRIM IS FRETSAWED OR JIGSAWED

INTO DECORATIVE SHAPES TO MAKE

ATTRACTIVE GABLE ENDS. A WATER

POT IS PUT INTO A HOLE IN THE

BASE. THIS VERSATILE AND

ATTRACTIVE FEEDER CAN BE EITHER

FREE STANDING OR ATTACHED TO A

WALL.

SUITABILITY

● Providing both food
and water, this
versatile feeder will
soon become known
to the local birds. This
is especially good for
winter feeding
because the roof
keeps rain and snow
off the seed. The joy
of this type of feeder
is that it caters to a
wide variety of
species – chickadees,
titmice, cardinals, jays,
doves, finches,
woodpeckers,
grosbeaks, and white-
crowned sparrows.
Experiment by adding
some different foods
to the staple diet and
see whether different
birds are attracted.
Pecan nuts, for
instance, are a
favorite of a number
of species, including
bluebirds, indigo
buntings, purple
finches, and wrens.

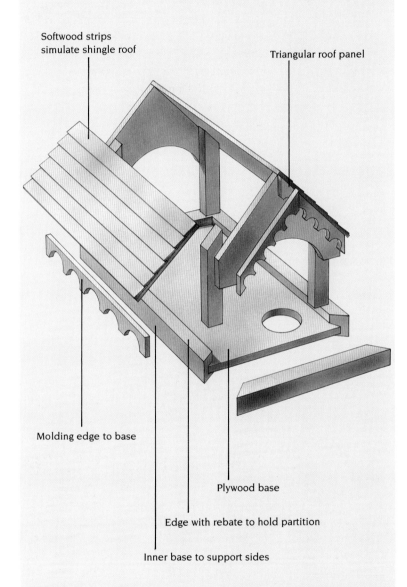

Softwood strips
simulate shingle roof

Triangular roof panel

Molding edge to base

Plywood base

Edge with rebate to hold partition

Inner base to support sides

1 Cut the base from the plywood board with a jigsaw.

2 Use a router or hand rabbet plane to form a rabbet on the 1¼ x 1in (30 x 25mm) wood strip and cut to fit the four sides of the base. Miter the edges for a neat join. The outer top edge of the strips may be bevelled with a plane or given a decorative molding with a router.

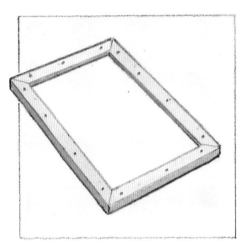

3 Attach the strips of edging to the base with brads and glue.

*This exploded diagram
shows how the
components fit together.
For the cutting
dimensions, see the
template on page 112.*

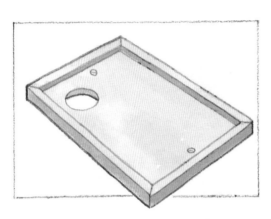

4 Cut out a hole for the water pot and drill out two drainage holes, one at each end.

5 Follow the template on page 112 or make a posterboard template of half an arch and form the complete arch shape by reversing the posterboard on the plywood.

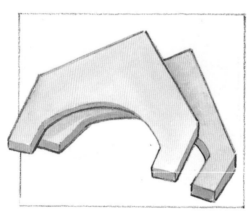

6 Use a jigsaw to cut out the two arched end pieces.

7 Cut the four post sections to size from the 1¼in square (30mm²) wood.

8 Cut out two sections of plywood for the roof and assemble the posts and arched end pieces.

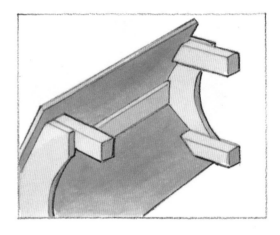

9 Attach a chamfered piece of softwood to the inside of the roof joint to add support.

10 Glue small curved decorative pieces to the external sides of each corner post, flush with the roof.

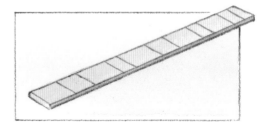

11 To make the shingle roof, make random light saw cuts across the thin roofing strips.

TURN YOUR CHALET INTO A MULTI-LEVEL FEEDING STATION BY ADDING HOOKS TO THE SIDE AND HANGING BAGS OF SEED.

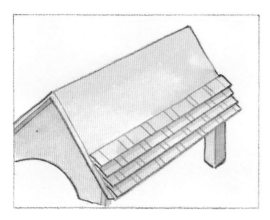

12 Attach the strips to the roof with brads and glue, adjusting each strip so that it lies parallel with the adjacent piece.

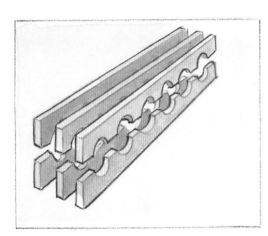

13 Make a repeating rounded pattern for the trim from posterboard and transfer this to the four softwood strips. Alternatively, make regularly spaced 1in (25mm) holes in a length of 2½ x 1in (62 x 25mm) softwood. Then slice the wood lengthways with a hand saw and cut the thin sections in half, across the holes, to give the semi-circle pattern.

14 Glue on small diamond shaped finials to each end of the roof.

The completed feeder would look good with the base, posts and decorative arched sections painted in your chosen color and the roof strips stained with a cedar-colored preservative.

THIS CHARMING SOUTHERN TOWNHOUSE IS GIVEN A TRADITIONAL AIR WITH PAINTED CLAPBOARD AND A TILED ROOF. THE CLAPBOARD APPEARANCE IS CREATED BY SHALLOW GROOVES CUT INTO THE WOOD WITH A BACKSAW, IN THE

SAVANNAH STYLE

SAME WAY AS THE DECKING FOR THE NOAH'S ARK (SEE PAGE 96). THE DOWNSTAIRS WINDOWS, THE FRONT DOOR AND THE PICKET FENCE ARE ALL MADE FROM SCRAPS OF SOLID WOOD GLUED TO THE STRUCTURE. THE DORMER WINDOWS AND THE SMALL FRONT PORCH ARE CHARMING FINISHING TOUCHES.

Shallow grooves cut using saw

Sides of house cut from MDF

Roof

Softwood dormer window

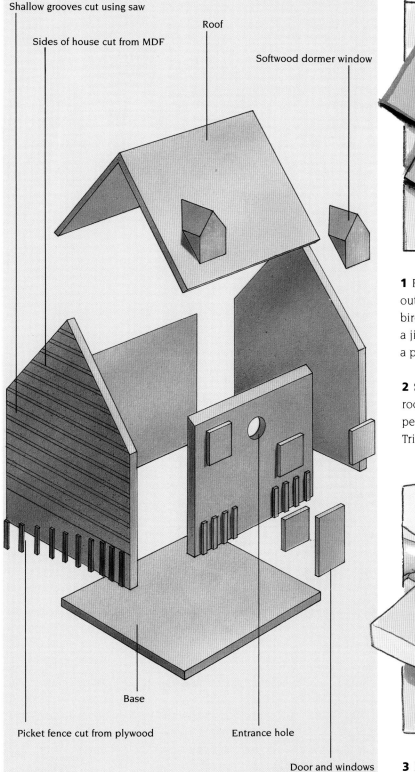

Base

Picket fence cut from plywood

Entrance hole

Door and windows
cut from plywood

*This exploded diagram
shows how the
components fit together.
For the cutting
dimensions, see the
template on page 113.*

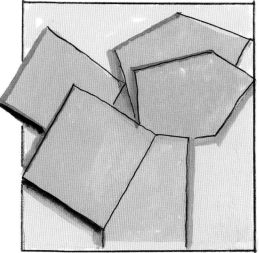

1 Following the template on page 113, lay out the back, sides, front, and base of the birdhouse on ⅝in (15mm) MDF. Cut out with a jigsaw and trim to pencil lines with a plane.

2 Set the sliding bevel to the slope of the roof. Using the set sliding bevel, lay out with pencil the angle on front and back portions. Trim to line with a plane.

3 Mark the position on the front portion for the entrance hole and cut out, using the drill with a 1¼in (30mm) spade bit.

4 Using a pencil or knife, lay out parallel horizontal lines approximately ⅜in (10mm) apart on the four sides of the birdhouse. Then cut shallow grooves with a backsaw, using a scrap piece of wood held in place with C-clamps as a guide.

5 Assemble the base and sides of the birdhouse using yellow glue and 1¼in (30mm) brads.

6 Lay out and cut with a jigsaw two pieces of ⅛in (4mm) plywood for the roof and trim edges with a plane.

7 On a 6in (150mm) length of 2 x 3in (50 x 75mm) softwood – finished size 1¾–2¼in (45–72mm) – lay out on either end the front shape of dormer window. Remove excess wood with a plane.

8 Using the already set sliding bevel, lay out roof angle and cut dormer with backsaw.

THE DESIGN OF THIS VICTORIAN COTTAGE BIRDHOUSE IS VERY CLOSE TO THAT OF THE SAVANNAH-STYLE BIRDHOUSE, THE DIFFERENCE LIES IN THE DECORATION AND THE ADDITION OF FEATURES.

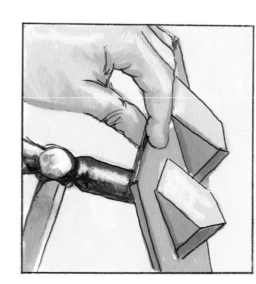

9 Glue and nail the dormer windows to one of the roof slopes, using ⅝in (15mm) brads. pins.

10 Glue and nail the roof into position.

11 On remaining plywood, lay out a rectangle for the door, squares for windows and strips for a picket fence. Cut out with a backsaw and sand the edges with medium grade grit sandpaper to remove all sawmarks.

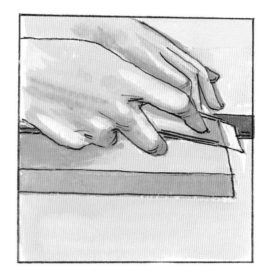

12 With a craft knife and a steel rule, cut vertical lines on the door to achieve a boarded effect.

13 Using medium grade grit sandpaper, thoroughly sand birdhouse and then glue on door, windows, and picket fence.

14 Apply one coat of primer paint, allow to dry, sand with fine grade grit sandpaper and then apply undercoat.

Paint the main body of
the birdhouse, windows
and roof in exterior paint
in the color of your
choice; then, using an
artist's brush and white
paint, carefully paint
squares to create a
window-pane effect.

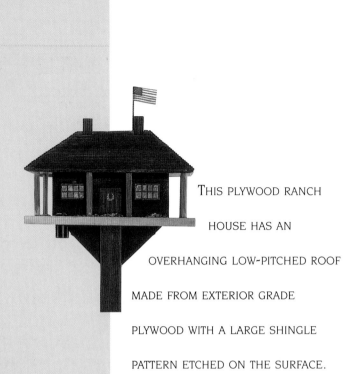

THIS PLYWOOD RANCH HOUSE HAS AN OVERHANGING LOW-PITCHED ROOF MADE FROM EXTERIOR GRADE PLYWOOD WITH A LARGE SHINGLE PATTERN ETCHED ON THE SURFACE. IT HAS A NARROW WRAPAROUND PORCH WITH POSTS TO SUPPORT THE ROOF. THE DOOR AND WINDOW

RANCH HOUSE

DETAILS ARE CREATED BY GLUING ON SMALL MOLDINGS AND THE WHOLE FEEDER STANDS ON A STOUT POST WITH SUPPORTS SCREWED UNDERNEATH. A SMALL WATER POT SITS IN A HOLE IN THE PORCH AND THE HOUSE IS PAINTED RED WITH A BUFF-COLORED ROOF.

SUITABILITY

● The narrow veranda part of this design ensures that only small birds, such as house finches, American goldfinches, nutchatches, and chickadees will feed here. Downy woodpeckers, however, can cling to the edge and sneak seeds, too. As with all birdfeeders, it is important that excess food and discarded seed husks are cleared regularly to prevent the table becoming infested by insects or a breeding ground for fungus and bacteria that can cause disease in birds.

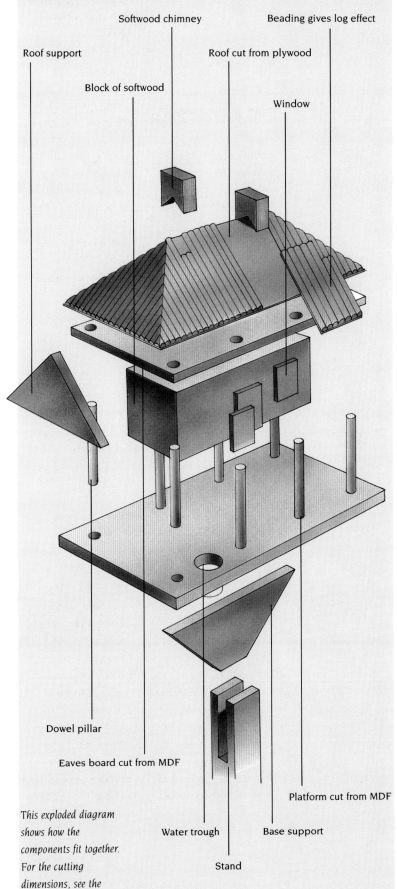

Roof support

Softwood chimney

Beading gives log effect

Roof cut from plywood

Block of softwood

Window

Dowel pillar

Eaves board cut from MDF

Water trough

Base support

Stand

Platform cut from MDF

This exploded diagram shows how the components fit together. For the cutting dimensions, see the template on page 114.

METHOD

1 Lay out, then use a jigsaw to cut two pieces of ⅝in (15mm) MDF for the platform and the eaves. Trim down to the line with a plane. For dimensions, see the template on page 114.

2 Lay out eight points on the platform, 1⅛in (32mm) from the edge. Place the eaves board on top of the platform and drill eight ½in (12.5mm) holes through both pieces.

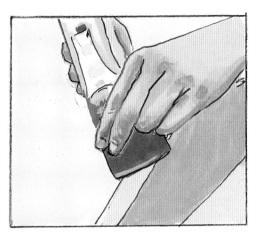

3 With a plane, bevel the edge of the eaves board all around to an angle of 45°. Test for accuracy with a miter square or sliding bevel set at 45°.

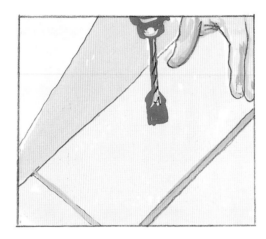

4 Using the electric drill fitted with a 1¼in (32mm) spade bit, make a hole in the platform for a water trough (plastic film canister).

5 Cut three pieces of ⅛in (3mm) plywood for the door and windows; glue and nail these to one side of the 10 x 4 x 4in (250 x 100 x 100mm) softwood.

7 Glue and assemble the eight lengths of dowel with the platform and the eaves. When the glue has set, use a plane to trim off the excess dowel that protrudes through the eaves.

6 Cut eight lengths of ½in (12.5mm) dowel to a length of 5⅛in (130mm) with a backsaw. Attach the piece of softwood block to the platform with yellow glue and brads.

THIS AMAZING CREATION IS A REPLICA OF A REAL BUILDING AND WAS MADE OF WOOD, METAL, AND MIRROR AND THEN PAINTED. IF THE RANCH HOUSE WERE BUILT AS A HOUSE, RATHER THAN AS A FEEDER WITH A SOLID BLOCK IN THE CENTER, IT COULD BE MADE TO LOOK SIMILAR TO THIS.

8 Cut two roof supports and a base support out of the remaining MDF, using a jigsaw. Finish the edges with a plane.

9 Cut out ⅛in (3mm) plywood for the roof; glue and nail in conjunction with the roof supports. Trim off any excess plywood with a plane. Cut two pieces of softwood for chimneys, 1¾ x 1¼ x ⅞in (40 x 30 x 22mm); cut out 45° V-shapes and glue to the roof. Use beading to give the roof a log effect.

10 Lay out and cut a vertical slot 4in deep and ⅝in wide (100mm and 15mm) in the base support/stand. Cut vertically with a backsaw and chop out the central section with a ⅝in (15mm) chisel. Spread glue in the slot and insert the base support.

11 When the glue on the base support/stand has set, drill two ³⁄₁₆in (5mm) holes in it and screw it to the underside of the platform.

12 Sand down with medium grade grit sandpaper, then apply two coats of wood stain preservative and decorate with a flag.

*You can use exterior quality paint
instead of wood preservative if desired.*

IF YOU WANT THE BIRDS

IN YOUR YARD TO NEST IN

STYLE, THIS GEORGIAN-

STYLE COUNTRY BIRDHOUSE IS IDEAL

WITH ITS PERFECTLY SYMMETRICAL

THREE STOREYS AND DOWEL

COLUMNS SUPPORTING THE PORCH.

THE DECORATIVE STONEWORK AT

MATERIALS

● 40in (1000mm) square piece of ½in (12.5mm) Exterior Grade MDF
● 16in (400mm²) square piece of ¾in (18mm) Exterior Grade MDF
● 12in square (300mm²) piece of ¼in (6mm) plywood
● 7in (175mm) length of ⅝in (15mm) hardwood dowel
● Scrap of roofing felt
● Brads
● Yellow glue
● Sandpaper
● Staples
● Exterior Grade paint

TOOLS

● Plane
● Hammer
● Jigsaw
● Backsaw
● Electric drill
● 1¼in (32mm) diameter spade bit
● Plane
● Brace
● ¾in (18mm) wood auger
● 1in (25mm) chisel
● Mallet
● Coarse file
● Paintbrushes
● Staple gun

COUNTRY HOUSE ''

THE CORNERS IS MADE FROM CUT-

OUT PIECES OF WOOD THE ROOF IS

MADE FROM EXTERNAL FELT, PINNED

INTO PLACE. THE STONE EFFECT ON

THE FAÇADE IS PRODUCED BY

ETCHING INTO THE SURFACE OF THE

BOARD AND THEN FINISHING IT

WITH SANDSTONE-COLORED

EXTERIOR PAINT.

SUITABILITY

● This relatively large birdhouse could attract a variety of different birds, depending upon the size of the entrance hole. This example has a single hole, measuring 1¼in (32mm) positioned 6in (150mm) above the base. This leaves a large nesting space suitable for the downy woodpecker, Bewick's wren, and tufted titmouse. A slightly smaller hole would suit the chickadees and wrens, and one that was a little larger could tempt swallows and bluebirds. If placed in a wooded area, and by making a 3in (75mm) entrance hole, you may attract a screech owl to roost or nest.

Decorative edging

Roof covered with roofing felt

Front roof peak

Blind hole

Sides of house cut from MDF

Door and windows
cut from MDF

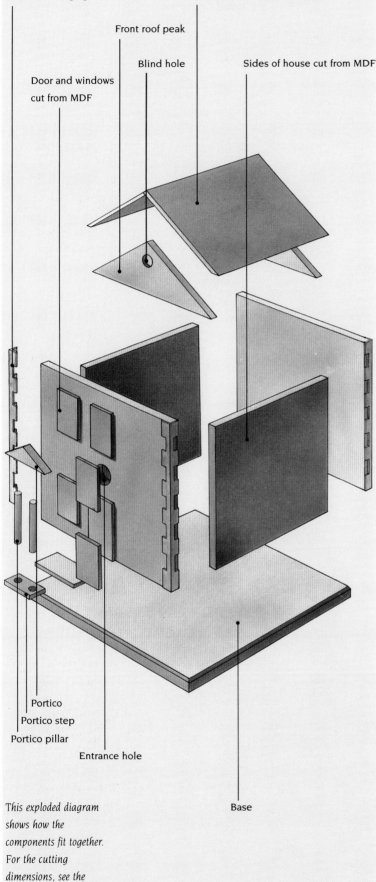

Portico

Portico step

Portico pillar

Entrance hole

Base

*This exploded diagram
shows how the
components fit together.
For the cutting
dimensions, see the
template on page 115.*

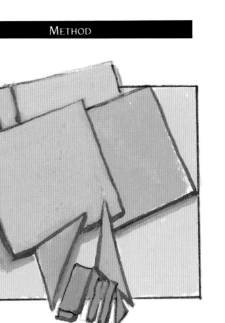

1 Following the template on page 115, lay out pieces for the base and portico roof from ¾in (18mm) MDF; the sides, front, back, and roof from ½in(12.5mm) MDF; the portico steps, window, and door from ¼in (6mm) MDF; the portico pillars 3½in (90mm) from ⅝in (15mm) dowel. Cut the MDF pretty close to the lines with a jigsaw and trim down to exact size with a plane. Cut the hardwood dowel with a backsaw.

2 Lay out the center of the front portion of the birdhouse; with an electric drill, fitted with a 1¼in (32mm) spade bit, drill a hole.

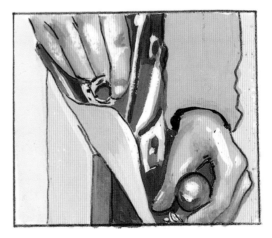

3 Chamfer three edges of the base with a plane.

4 Assemble all sides and roof by gluing and nailing together.

5 In the center of the front roof peak drill a blind hole (one that does not go right through) with an ¾in (18mm) auger bit fitted to a brace. (An electric drill can be very difficult to control and might pull straight through.)
6 Thoroughly sand the birdhouse and the edges of the steps, door, and window with medium grade grit sandpaper.

7 From the remaining ¼in (6mm) plywood, cut eight strips ¾ x 12in (18mm x 300mm) using a jigsaw fitted with a fine blade; trim to precise size with a plane.

AN EXACT REPLICA OF THE HISTORIC MOORE HOUSE IN YORKTOWN, VIRGINIA, THIS BIRDHOUSE EMPLOYS A BASIC SQUARE SHAPE, BUT HAS BEEN FINISHED WITH GREAT ATTENTION TO DETAIL.

8 With a pencil, mark steps at 1⅛in (30mm) intervals to a depth of ⅜in (9mm) (half way); make cuts with a backsaw and chop out with a 1in (25mm) chisel and mallet. Use a coarse file to smooth out any irregularities in the steps.

9 Apply glue and attach this plywood to the corners of the birdhouse with a heavy duty staple gun or brads.

10 Apply glue to the door and windows and staple or nail them into position.

11 Assemble the portico by gluing and nailing the steps into the dowel end from underneath, and also from the top.

12 Glue and nail the portico into position around the door.

13 Cut roofing felt with a craft knife and staple or nail it to the roof.

14 Apply primer paint, undercoat and the finishing color to the bird house, lightly sanding down between each coat with fine sandpaper.

15 Highlight window detail by painting in black with a No. 6 artist's brush.

If several pairs nest in this grand birdhouse, you will know you've made them truly welcome.

- 3ft 3in (1m) square of ½in (12.5mm) Exterior Grade MDF or plywood
- 18in (460mm) of ¼in (6.5mm) hardwood dowel
- 10in (25cm) of ½in square (12.5mm²) hardwood
- Brads
- Yellow glue
- No 6 plated countersunk woodscrews
- Sandpaper

- Backsaw
- Jigsaw
- Try square
- 1in (25mm) and 1½in (38mm) hole saws
- Router
- Rabbet plane
- C-clamps
- Plane
- Electric drill and assorted bits
- Drill stand
- Hammer
- Screwdriver
- Paintbrushes

THIS VERY GOOD-LOOKING, RATHER VERTICAL TWO-STOREY NEST BOX WITH ITS TWO ENTRANCE HOLES WILL ATTRACT BOTH SMALL AND LARGE BIRDS, AND THERE MAY BE AN INTERESTING TUSSLE FOR OWNERSHIP. THE SCHOOLHOUSE CAN BE MADE FROM EXTERIOR GRADE MDF OR PLYWOOD,

NEW ENGLAND SCHOOLHOUSE

PAINTED TO PROTECT IT FROM THE WEATHER. THE CLAPBOARD EFFECT IS CREATED BY CUTTING SHALLOW HORIZONTAL GROOVES WITH A BACKSAW.

SUITABILITY

- By varying the size of the entrance hole and where it is placed, this birdhouse will suit different species. Make the hole 2in (50mm) and it would be great for a red-bellied or red-headed woodpecker, though also attractive to starlings. A slightly smaller hole 1½in (38mm) is suitable for a hairy or downy woodpecker. Keep in mind that excavating a nest cavity is an important part of woodpecker courtship behavior. If you want to attract woodpeckers, fill the box with wood chips to give them material to excavate. The 1½in (38mm) hole would also be attractive to violet-green and tree swallows, titmice, and bluebirds.

Upper entrance hole

Top roof

Main roof

V-shape section

Balustrade made from dowel

Shallow grooves
cut with a saw

*This exploded diagram
shows how the
components fit together.
For the cutting
dimensions, see the
template on page 116.*

Base

Lower entrance hole

METHOD

1 Using the template given on page 116, lay out the main parts of the birdhouse on the MDF or plywood sheet and cut them out roughly with the jigsaw. Trim back to the pencil lines with a plane.

2 Draw parallel, horizontal lines in pencil and then cut shallow grooves in the wall pieces with a backsaw, using a scrap strip of wood as a guide, held in place with C-clamps.

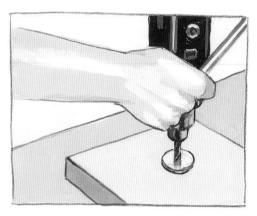

3 For cutting the bird entry holes, clamp the front of the birdhouse to the drill stand with a piece of scrap wood underneath and drill with the relevant size bit or hole saw. Use a router fitted with a self-guiding rabbet bit cutter to cut a step around each opening.

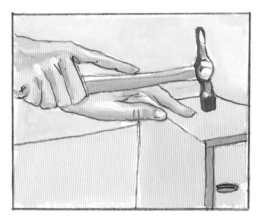

4 Glue and nail all the sides of the birdhouse together using a waterproof Exterior Grade yellow glue. Attach the roof and glue and nail it into position.

5 Lay out the top section of the birdhouse and cut the sides with a backsaw, trimming back to the lines with a plane. Cut the V-shaped section accurately with a backsaw.

6 Following the instructions for step 3, drill another entry hole in this section if required. Then glue and nail to assemble.

7 Attach the small house on top of the large one. Glue and nail the top house to the lower one from the inside, then attach the roof on the top house.

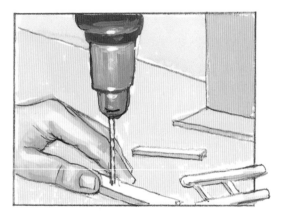

8 Using a fine-toothed saw, cut the ¼in (6mm) dowel and the ½ x ½in (12.5 x 12.5mm) hardwood into the lengths given on the template on page 116 to make the balustrade. Use a ¼in (6mm) drill to make holes in the uprights to take the dowelling.

Add a small bell tower, a sign, and a flag and almost any birdhouse can be transformed into a school. Of course, the classes would be very small and the lessons may be how to fly rather than how to read and write.

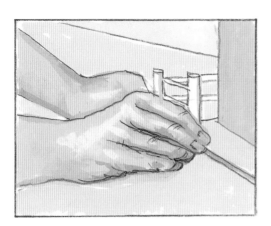

9 Sand all parts of the birdhouse. Assemble the balustrade, gluing, then tapping the dowelling into place.

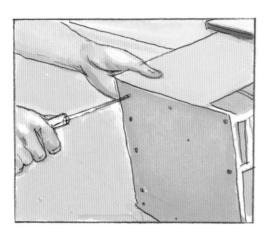

10 Assemble all the parts of the birdhouse, using No. 6 plated screws to withstand outdoor conditions.

11 Finish off the outside by painting with Exterior Grade undercoat, then a flat finish top coat of paint. This is preferable to gloss paint since it is less reflective.

The double-decker schoolhouse with two nesting boxes – one for small birds, the other for bigger species – makes an attractive and interesting home. You may be lucky and get two different types of bird nesting at the same time.

DERIVED FROM

MEXICAN CHURCH

ARCHITECTURE, THIS

BIRDHOUSE IS A NEST BOX FOR BIRDS

THAT LIKE A WIDE OPENING. ITS

ROUGH RENDERED EXTERIOR IS

SIMPLY CRAFTED, AND TRADITIONAL

COLORS OF FINISHING ARE PASTEL

YELLOW OR PINK.

THE RECTANGULAR DESIGN HAS

CRENELLATED DETAIL AT THE BACK

MATERIALS

● 30in (750mm)
square piece of No. 6
⅜in (9mm) Exterior
Grade plywood
● 20in (500mm)
length of ⅜in (9mm)
hardwood dowel
● Brads
● Brass eyelet and
hook
● Scraps of softwood
● Sand
● Yellow glue
● Exterior paint
● Sandpaper

TOOLS

● Panel or circular
saw
● Drill
● ⅜in (9mm) auger bit
● Fretsaw or jigsaw
● Hammer
● Tape measure
● Try square

MISSION CHURCH

AND THE FRONT, A CROSS AT THE

REAR AND A SMALL BELL INSET AT

THE FRONT. THE CARCASS AND THE

DOORS ARE MADE FROM PLYWOOD.

SUITABILITY

● This slot-sided
design will attract
flycatchers, robins,
and phoebes who like
to nest in an open
box. The birdhouse
should be positioned
in a secluded location,
perhaps deep in the
fork of a tree or
secured in a high
thick hedge, about
6–15ft (2–4.5m) off
the ground. If you
open the entire side,
so that the opening
measures
approximately 10 x
4in (250 x 100mm),
you would be even
more likely to attract
these birds, which use
a platform-type,
rather than a cavity,
nester.

Flat roof

Cross

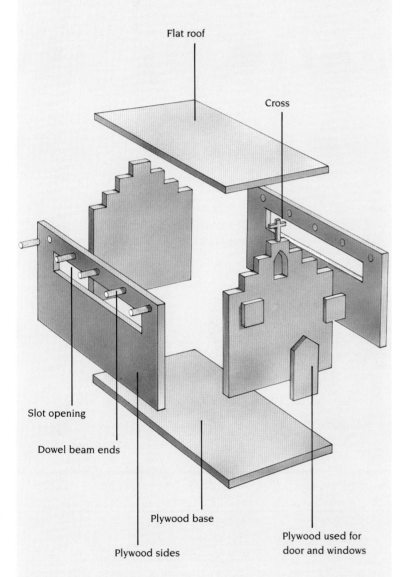

Slot opening

Dowel beam ends

Plywood base

Plywood sides

Plywood used for
door and windows

*This exploded diagram
shows how the
components fit together.
For the cutting
dimensions, see the
template on page 117*

1 Cut front, back, sides, base, and roof out of
the plywood following the template on page
117. Use a panel saw for the straight edges
and a fretsaw or jigsaw for the stepped tops
of the front and back.

2 Clean up all the rough edges with medium
grade grit sandpaper.

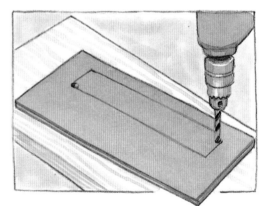

3 Lay out the measurements for the 11 x
1½in (280 x 38mm) slit opening on one side.
Make a starter hole in one corner of the
marked area with a drill bit.

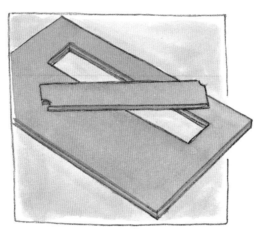

4 Clamp a straight piece of plywood to the side to act as a guide, and cut the slit opening using a jigsaw.

5 Drill 12 holes in the base for drainage.

6 Mark positions for the dowels along both sides.

THIS MORE USUAL STYLE OF CHURCH MAKES AN EQUALLY GOOD BIRDHOUSE, ALTHOUGH DIFFERENT SPECIES WILL BE ATTRACTED TO THE TYPE WITH A HOLE RATHER THAN A SIDE SLOT ENTRANCED.

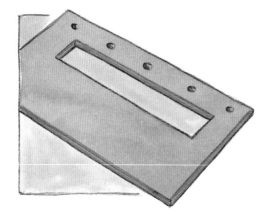

7 Place scrap plywood under the sides and drill the holes for the dowels.

8 Lay out the measurements of the bell recess on the plywood following the template.

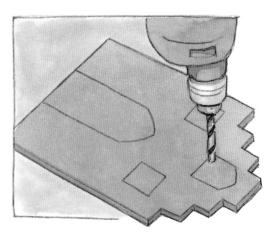

9 Make a starter hole as in Step **3** in one corner of the layed out bell and cut out the shape with a jigsaw.

10 Cut out the plywood dummy side windows, the front windows and the arched door to the measurements on the template.

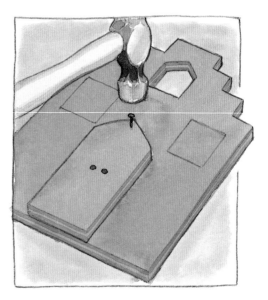

11 Glue and nail the windows and door into place, making sure they are symmetrical.

15 Tap one 1¾in (40mm) section of dowel into each side hole. These make the roof beams.

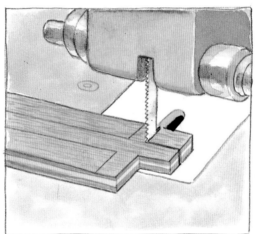

16 Cut out the small plywood cross with a fretsaw or jigsaw following the template shape traced on the wood.

17 Cut off the head of a brad, and use both ends of the brad to attach the cross to the top of the back wall.

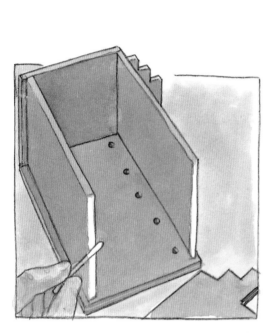

12 Assemble the church using brads, and apply yellow glue along all meeting edges.

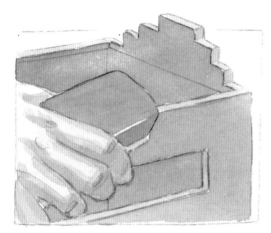

13 Smooth the top of the visible plywood with sandpaper to level all the top edges.

14 Cut 12 1¾in (40mm) long pieces of ⅜in (9mm) dowel.

THE MISSION CHURCH IS AN ELABORATE VARIATION OF TRADITIONAL SLOT ENTRANCE BIRDHOUSE. THIS EXAMPLE WAS MADE USING CEDAR, A PARTICULARLY ATTRACTIVE WOOD.

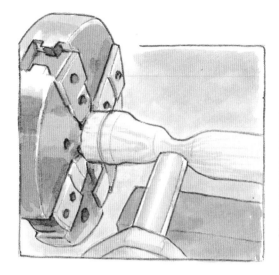

18 Shape a bell from a piece of softwood, following the template. Alternatively, turn it on a lathe.

19 Attach the bell to the front of the church with the brass eyelet and hook.

20 Coat the sides and top with a diluted yellow glue solution and, before it is anywhere near dry, sprinkle sand evenly over the surface.

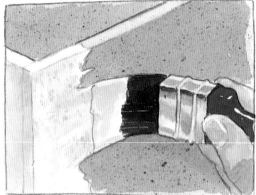

21 Brush wood preservative on to the base of the box.

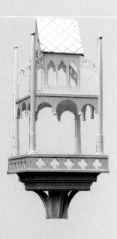

AN INTRICATE BIRD TABLE IN NINETEENTH-CENTURY GOTHIC STYLE.

The rough rendered exterior of the nester can be finished by painting it in the traditional mission church colors of pastel yellow or pink — or you can choose any other color you may prefer. Although you could use the roof as a feeder, remember that this will deter birds from nesting.

THIS PRETTY BRITISH

THATCHED-ROOF COTTAGE

HAS A DECIDEDLY OLD-FASHIONED

FEEL TO IT AND BLENDS WELL INTO A

GARDEN ENVIRONMENT. THE

BIRDHOUSE IS MADE FROM A BASIC

WOOD FRAME WITH ADDED

MOLDINGS TO REPRESENT THE

MATERIALS

● 4ft square
(1200mm²) piece of
¼in (6mm) Exterior
Grade MDF
● Pieces of ⅜in (9mm)
Exterior Grade MDF,
approx 5 x 10in
(125 x 250mm)
● Strips of ⅜in square
(9mm²) hardwood
plus 4 x 3in (100 x
75mm) rectangle for
the door
● Roofing felt
● Yellow glue
● Exterior paint
● Brads
● Sandpaper

TOOLS

● Jigsaw
● Electric drill
● Hammer
● Craft knife
● Try square
● Tape measure and
pencil
● Hand plane
● Paintbrushes

TUDOR COTTAGE

BEAMS. THE SMALL PORCH AT THE

FRONT FORMS THE ENTRANCE FOR

THE BIRDS AND THE WINDOWS ARE

SMALL AND ALSO MADE FROM

MOLDINGS.

SUITABILITY

● The design of this
birdhouse and the
location of the hole
means that birds can
only nest in the porch
area of the structure,
which makes it
suitable for many
small birds. Place this
nesting box in
relatively open
ground, but near
trees, for house
wrens, bluebirds,
titmice, and
chickadees. Tree
swallows are
particularly attracted
to areas with open
water.

1 Following the template on page 118, lay out all the components of the house on the sheet of MDF, being careful to make the sides parallel with a try square. Lay out the two sides of the porch on the scrap of thicker MDF.

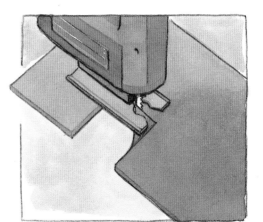

2 Cut out each part, remembering to cut out the opening between the porch and the main structure on the front section if you wish to attract larger birds. Drill entrance hole in front section of the porch.

3 Nail and glue the bottom, sides, and front of the house together and set aside to dry. Check that the corners are at 90° with the try square.

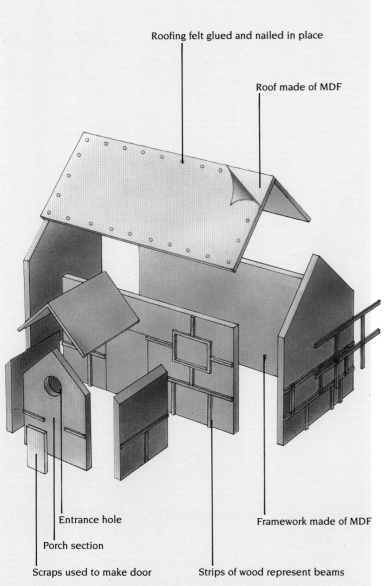

Roofing felt glued and nailed in place

Roof made of MDF

Entrance hole

Porch section

Scraps used to make door

Framework made of MDF

Strips of wood represent beams

This exploded diagram shows how the components fit together. For the cutting dimensions, see the template on page 118.

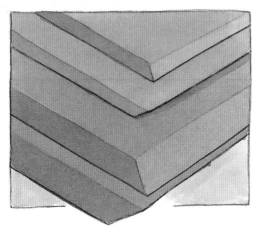

4 Chamfer the top edges of the front and back of the building and the top edges of the porch sides.

5 Attach the porch sides to the front wall with yellow glue and two brads per side.

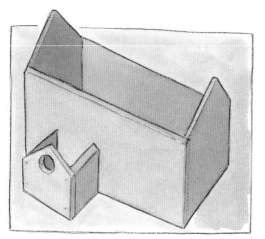

6 Glue and nail the front of the porch in place before painting the exterior of the house in your chosen color. This should be a neutral tone to mimic the original's wattle and daub or flat white.

7 Attach the roof sections of the porch and main house in the same way. One edge overlaps the other at the apex to form a neat joint.

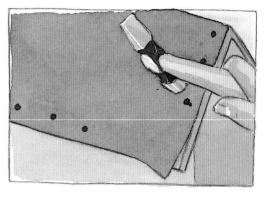

8 Nail on the thin roofing felt and trim the edges to give an exact fit over the MDF pieces of roof. Space the brads at approximately 1in (25mm) intervals.

A THATCHED ROOF ADDS A RUSTIC FEEL TO A BIRDHOUSE AND EVOKES AN "OLDE WORLDE" CHARM.

9 The last stage of the structure is to nail and glue small pieces of the hardwood molding around the walls to represent beams. Use a craft knife to chamfer the outside edges of the molding before cutting it to the required length. Add a thin section for the front door.

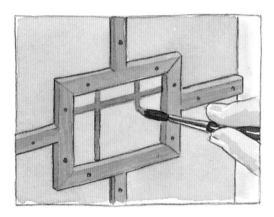

10 Paint the beams flat black and paint on more decorative detail, such as windows, with a small artist's brush.

This "olde worlde" design birdhouse would look just right in a cottage-type yard or garden, full of old-fashioned plants and rambling roses. The thatched roof was made by attaching twigs with glue and thin wire.

THIS ELEGANT COLONIAL

BIRDHOUSE HAS A

PERFECTLY SYMMETRICAL SHAPE.

THE TALL CENTRAL SPIRE AND THE

TWO SMALLER OUTER ONES ARE

MADE FROM SOLID WOOD AND ARE

PLANED TO GIVE PYRAMID POINTS.

THE CLASSICAL STYLE IS CONTINUED

IN THE LARGE RECTANGULAR

WINDOWS, THE DOWEL COLUMNS

MATERIALS

- 20in square (500mm²) piece of ¾in (18mm) Exterior Grade MDF
- 12in square (300mm²) piece of ¼in (6mm) Exterior Grade MDF
- 8 x 1⅛ x 1⅜in (200 x 30 x 35mm) piece of softwood
- 6 x 1⅛ x 1¾in (150 x 30 x 45mm) piece of softwood
- 10in (250mm) length of ⅞in (22mm) hardwood dowel
- Yellow glue
- Brads
- Sandpaper
- Exterior Grade paint

TOOLS

- Try square
- Jigsaw
- Plane
- Hammer
- Backsaw
- Bracing board
- Awl
- Chisel
- Electric drill
- 1¼in (32mm) spade bit
- Paintbrushes
- Pencil

NEOCLASSICAL NESTER ////

AND THE PROTRUDING PORCH. THE

PORTICO ABOVE THE PORCH HOUSES

THE ENTRY INTO THE BIRDHOUSE.

THE WHITE-PAINTED FINISH

COMPLETES THE COLONIAL LOOK.

SUITABILITY

- As with most birdhouses, the size of the hole determines which birds will nest in it. The large internal space enclosed by this nesting box makes it suitable for several species, including the bluebird. The decline in the numbers of these beautiful creatures has been reversed over the last 10–15 years by people erecting backyard birdhouses. It is, however, critical that the hole is exactly 1½in (38mm) to prevent the use of the box by starlings. Bluebirds prefer boxes 5–6ft (1.5–1.8m) high that are sited in field-type locations. There can be some scattered trees, but not a permanently shaded area.

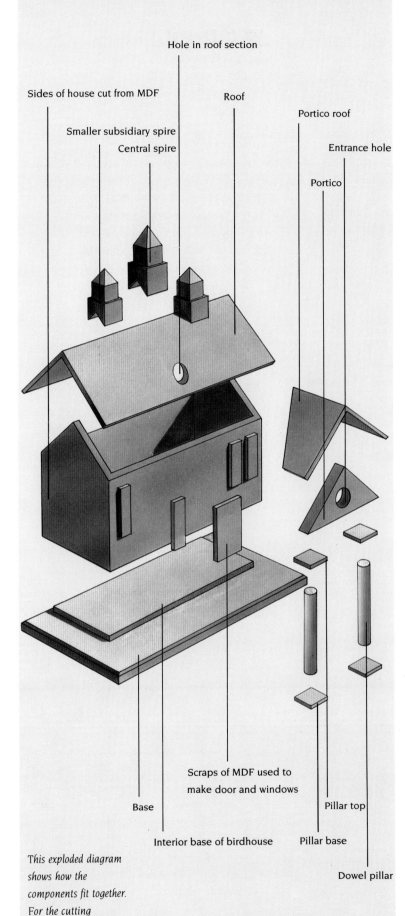

Hole in roof section

Sides of house cut from MDF

Roof

Portico roof

Smaller subsidiary spire

Entrance hole

Central spire

Portico

Scraps of MDF used to
make door and windows

Base

Pillar top

Interior base of birdhouse

Pillar base

Dowel pillar

*This exploded diagram
shows how the
components fit together.
For the cutting
dimensions, see the
template on page 119.*

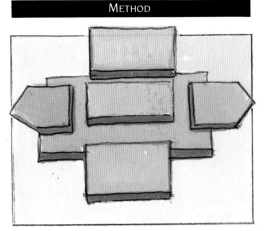

1 On the ¾in (18mm) MDF lay out the base
14 x 7½in (350 x 190mm), the bottom 11½ x
5⅛in (295 x 130mm), two sides 11½ x 5⅛in
(295 x 130mm) and two ends 5⅛ x 7⅜in (130 x
195mm) of the birdhouse (lay out the two
ends so that the peak forms a 90° angle). Cut
slightly oversize with a jigsaw and trim to
lines with a plane.

2 Use a plane to chamfer three edges of the
base, and sand smooth.

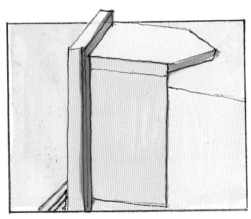

3 Glue and nail all these pieces together.

4 When the glue has set, trim off any
irregularities with a plane.

5 Lay out and cut two pieces of ¼in (6mm) MDF for the roof, trim to 4⅜ x 12¼ in (110 x 310mm) with a plane and then glue and nail these to the main body of the birdhouse.

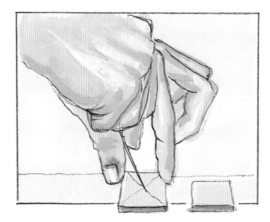

6 On the ¼in (6mm) MDF lay out the four small squares 1⅜ x 1⅜in (35 x 35mm) for the pillar bases and tops. Cut with a backsaw and then smooth off the edges with medium grit sandpaper. Draw diagonal lines to find the center and make an indentation with an awl.

7 With a backsaw and a bracing board, cut two pieces of ⅞in (22mm) dowel 4½in (115mm) long. Then glue and nail the pillar bases to the dowel.

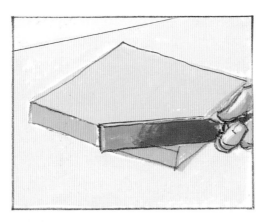

8 Chamfer the pillar bases and tops with a chisel.

9 From the remaining ¼in (6mm) MDF cut a piece for the door 2 x 3⅛in (50 x 80mm) and four ¾ x 2¾in (18 x 72mm) pieces for the window. Glue and nail the door into position but leave the windows.

10 From a scrap of ¾in (18mm) MDF, cut a triangle 4 x 5⅛in (100 x 130mm) from the top of the portico. Sand the edges; mark the middle and make a hole with an electric drill fitted with a 1¼in (32mm) spade bit. Tidy up the inside of the hole with sandpaper, sand any marks left by the spade bit.

11 Assemble the portico by gluing and nailing.

12 Mark and cut two angled pieces of ¼in (6mm) MDF for the portico roof 3⅜ x 4in (85 x 100mm); glue and nail these into position.

13 Glue and nail windows into position.

14 From the two pieces of softwood, cut the wood for the spires; two 3½in (90mm) long from the thinner piece and one 5in (125mm) long from the thicker. Mark out 90° V-shapes on them and cut away with a backsaw, so that they sit precisely on top of the roof. With a pencil mark in ¼in (6mm) half way up the spires and reduce the width with the backsaw to create a stepped effect.

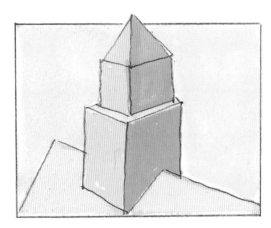

15 Mark lines for a pyramid point, cut with backsaw, and glue and nail these to the roof.

16 Using a medium grade grit sandpaper remove any saw marks.

The house can be finished by painting in a color of your choice.

THIS TRADITIONAL WINDMILL DESIGN COMBINES FEEDER AND NEST BOX. IT CAN BE PLACED AT ANY HEIGHT ON A STOUT WOODEN POST WITH AN ALUMINUM CONE NEAR THE BOTTOM OF THE POST TO DETER FOUR-FOOTED PREDATORS. THE FEEDER PART OF THIS BIRDHOUSE HAS A FOOD HOLE WITH WIRE MESH ACROSS IT, IMITATING THE CENTER DOOR OF A WINDMILL, AND A SHALLOW DRINKING TROUGH ON THE BASE. THE ROOF LIFTS TO MAKE THE

MATERIALS

- Quarter panel 2 x 4ft (600 x 1200mm) No. 6 ⅜in (9mm) Exterior Grade plywood
- One-eighth panel 2ft square (600mm²) No. 4 ¼in (6mm) Exterior Grade plywood
- 6 x 6 x 1in (150 x 150 x 25mm) piece of pine
- 4in (100mm) length of ¼in (6mm) dowel
- Plastic lid to fit grooved hole 3in (75mm) diameter
- 3⅛ x 4in (80 x 100mm) piece of galvanized wire mesh
- Bowl to fit in hole 3½in (90mm) diameter
- Four No. 6 ¾in (18mm) countersunk plated wood screws

- Brads
- Staples
- 2in (50mm) plated flush hinge and No. 4 ½in (12.5mm) screws
- Yellow glue
- Sandpaper
- ¾in (18mm) long piece of 1in (25mm) dowel (or old broom handle) for the spacer
- One No. 10 2in (50mm) japanned round head screw
- 6in (150mm) square piece of roofing lead
- Exterior primer
- Exterior paint

WINDY MILLER

FOOD AREA FILLABLE, AND TWO PERCHING POSTS UNDER THE WIRE MESH PREVENT THE SAILS TURNING AND POSSIBLY HARMING ONE OF YOUR FEATHERED FRIENDS. THE DOOR ON THE GROUND FLOOR IS ALWAYS OPEN TO VISITORS.

TOOLS

- Jigsaw
- Plane
- Pair of compasses
- Sliding bevel
- Electric drill and bit
- Craft knife
- Awl
- Screwdriver
- Coarse rasp or plane
- Metal snips
- Paintbrushes
- Metal ruler

SUITABILITY

- This creation could be a multi-purpose structure, feeder up top and nesting box on the bottom. This large opening would attract starlings, a smaller hole would attract smaller birds. Often, however, nesting birds will fly into a rage if they hear feeding birds singing nearby (in this case, upstairs). You could, of course, play it safe and turn the ground floor into a feeder as well, by fitting mesh to the door.

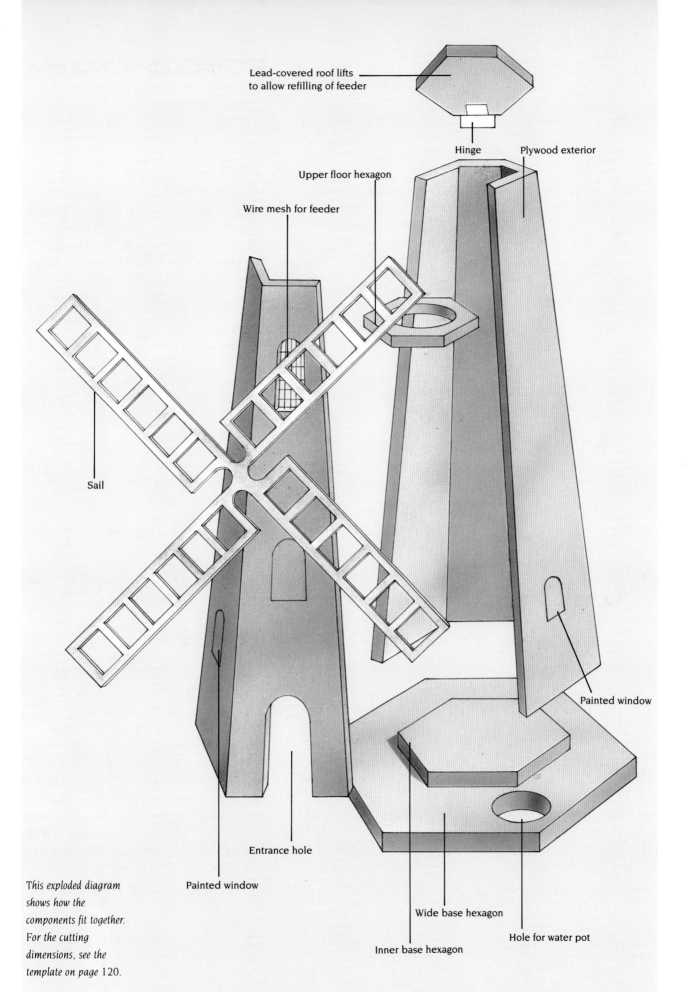

Lead-covered roof lifts
to allow refilling of feeder

Hinge

Plywood exterior

Upper floor hexagon

Wire mesh for feeder

Sail

Painted window

Entrance hole

Painted window

Wide base hexagon

Hole for water pot

Inner base hexagon

*This exploded diagram
shows how the
components fit together.
For the cutting
dimensions, see the
template on page 120.*

METHOD

1 Following the template on page 120 or by using a pair of compasses, lay out three circles on ⅜in (9mm) plywood to the following measurements: two 4¾in (120mm) in diameter for top and the second floor; one 9¾in (240mm) in diameter for the ground floor; and one 20in (500mm) in diameter for the base.

2 Once the circle is measured, use the radius to mark off each side of the hexagon. Cut out each hexagon with a jigsaw, and trim each to line with a plane.

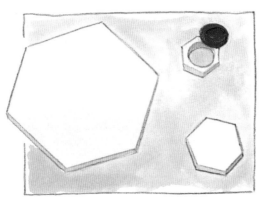

3 On the base hexagon, use a pair of compasses to lay out a circle which is slightly smaller in diameter than the drinking bowl. The circle in our model is 3½in (90mm) in diameter. Drill a starter hole inside the circle and cut out with a jigsaw.

4 Lay and cut out a circular hole in the second floor for the plastic feeding tray following the instructions in Step **3**. The plastic lid in our model fits a hole 3in (75mm) in diameter.

5 Lay out six side pieces on ⅜in (9mm) plywood to the following measurements: 24in (600mm) tall, 4½in (113mm) at the base and 2½in (65mm) at the top.

6 Set your sliding bevel to 60° and, with a pencil, mark the angles on the top and the bottom of the side pieces, and then trim them to the angle with a plane.

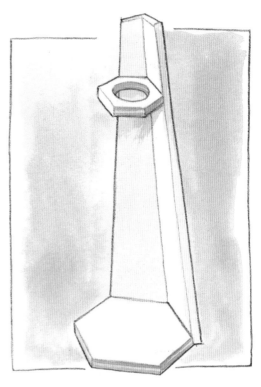

7 Glue and nail two sides to the ground floor and the first floor.

8 While the glue is setting, lay out the window and door on ⅜in (9mm) plywood and cut these out with a jigsaw.

9 Attach wire mesh to the inside of the window using staples. *Optional*: to attach the mesh flush to the outside of the window, cut it into shape and attach it with staples (you may need very fine mesh to shape it accurately); alternatively, to shape the mesh, bend it around the inside of the window, and fasten it from the back.

15 Lay out a 2½in (65mm) diameter hexagon on the pine for the roof.

16 Cut out the roof with a jigsaw and round off the top edge with a coarse rasp or a plane.

17 Cut the lead into a rough circle 3¼in (80mm) in diameter with metal snips.

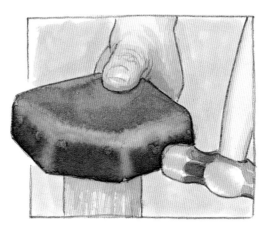

10 Glue and nail the remaining sides one at a time to the ground floor and second floor and to each other. Hold the tops together with a staple. A rubber band or masking tape are useful clamping aids.

11 When all the glue has set, smooth down the whole work using sandpaper.

18 Hammer the lead into the shape of the roof. This is best done gradually, by working your way around the shape.

19 When the lead roof is completely formed, cut off the excess and secure the lead to the roof with brads.

12 Using an awl and a metal rule as a guide, score parallel lines on all the sides to achieve a wood-clad effect.

13 Smooth the base hexagon.

14 Attach the base to the underside of the birdhouse with four No. 6 ¾in (18mm) countersunk plated wood screws.

24 Cut out the vanes with a jigsaw fitted with a fine blade. If necessary, finish off the edges with a coarse file.

25 Drill a hole in the center of the vanes and in the center of the 1in (25mm) spacer.

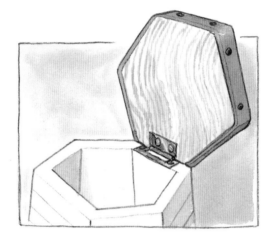

20 Attach the 2in (50mm) plated flush hinge to the roof with the No. 4 ½in (12.5mm) screws.

21 Drill two holes ¼in (6mm) in diameter under the window.

22 Put a drop of glue in the holes and insert one 2in (50mm) length of ¼in (6mm) dowel into each hole.

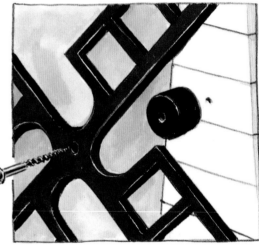

26 Attach the vanes and the spacer to the center of the front side of the birdhouse with a No. 10 2in (50mm) coated round head screw.

27 Finish the birdhouse by painting with Exterior Grade gloss.

Paint the finished windmill first with Exterior Grade primer, second with undercoat and third with gloss. We have painted the main body in white and the wind vanes and imitation windows in black, since they are traditional colors. Other colors may be more suitable for the color scheme and design of your yard.

MADE USING WOOD, METAL, AND FIBERGLASS, THIS FEEDER IS SURE TO TEMPT ANY PASSING BIRDS.

23 Using the template, draw the silhouette of the wind vanes (sails) on the veneer core plywood. Mark the outline precisely with a craft knife.

THE SQUARE-SIDED TOWER WITH ITS STEEPLY PITCHED ROOF DOMINATES THE APPEARANCE OF THIS GOTHIC MANSION. IN FACT, IT IS ONLY THE TOWER THAT IS USED AS A NEST BOX, THOUGH FURTHER NESTING AREAS COULD BE MADE IN THE REST OF THE BUILDING BY OPENING UP OTHER ENTRANCES AND MAKING PARTITIONS

GOTHIC MANSION

INSIDE. THE WINDOWS ARE ALL MADE BY CUTTING OUT THE POINTED GOTHIC ARCH AND GLUING ON A FALSE BLANK PIECE INSIDE — PAINTED BLACK TO GIVE THE HOUSE A SUITABLY HAUNTED EFFECT.

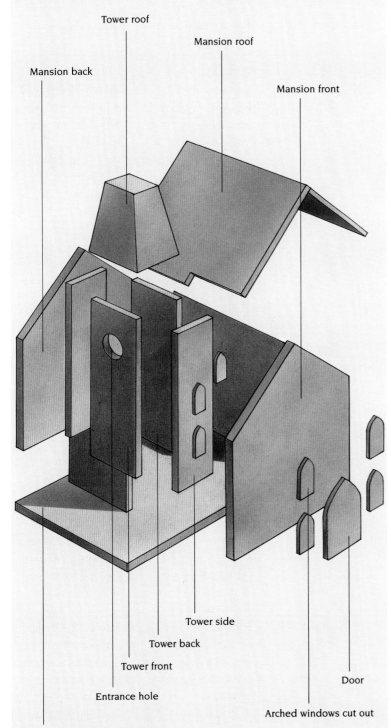

Tower roof

Mansion roof

Mansion back

Mansion front

Tower side

Tower back

Tower front

Door

Entrance hole

Arched windows cut out

Base cut from MDF

1 Following the template on page 121, lay out the castle sections on the ⅜in (9mm) MDF sheet and cut out with a panel saw or circular saw. Sand smooth any rough cut edges.

2 Do the same with the ¾in (18mm) MDF which will be used as the base.

This exploded diagram shows how the components fit together. For the cutting dimensions, see the template on page 121.

PAINTED IN DARK, SOMBER COLORS, THIS HOUSE CAN BE MADE TO LOOK HAUNTED. EXPERIMENT WITH COLOR SCHEMES ON YOUR BIRDHOUSES AND SEE THE DIFFERENCE THEY MAKE.

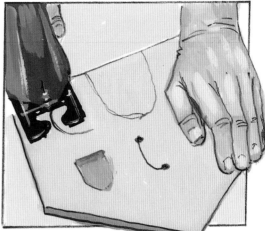

4 Cut out the windows with a jigsaw or fretsaw. Use a drill and drill bit to make pilot holes for each window. The circular 1¼in (32mm) diameter entrance hole at the side of the tower should also be cut out at this stage. This is 7in (175mm) above the level of the base.

3 Next, mark the positions of the arched window shapes on the front of the castle and tower. These are 2¾in (72mm) high and 1¼in (32mm) wide on the house and 1½in (38mm) high by ¾in (18mm) wide on the tower. Use a poster board template to make sure that the windows are all the same shape.

5 To give the appearance of weather-board cladding, use a backsaw guided by a straight edge to make shallow cuts at ⅝in (15mm) intervals horizontally across the walls.

6 Paint the front of the tower and castle with the eggshell paint, giving the birdhouse a distressed gray appearance. Painting these sections at this stage means that the inside edges of the windows can be coated before the inner plastic sheet is added.

7 Staple a section of black plastic sheeting to the back of the window areas. The piece on the inside of the tower should be 2in (50mm) wide and about 7in (175mm) long. The larger piece needed to blacken the castle windows should be cut 9in (225mm) wide and 7in (175mm) high. Plywood could be used as an alternative to plastic.

INSPIRED BY A GOTHIC FOLLY, THIS BIRDFEEDER WOULD BE A STYLISH AND ATTRACTIVE ADDITION TO ANY YARD.

8 Assemble the walls of the castle on the base using brads and glue.

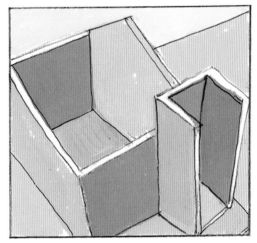

9 Add the tower, again with brads and glue. Nail a square block of scrap MDF at the base of the tower to hold each of the walls square at the base.

10 After painting the rest of the walls, add the two 7 x 8½in (175mm x 215mm) roof sections, nailing and gluing them in place. The MDF sections overlap at the apex and the left-hand piece is shaped to fit around the tower at its edge.

11 To make the top of the tower, plane the softwood block to make a steeply sloping roof. The finished height is 4½in (115mm) and the top should be 3in (75mm) wide and 2in (50mm) deep.

12 Smooth the wood with sandpaper and center the roof on the top of the tower, attaching with yellow glue.

13 Cut out the shaped 7in (175mm) long trim with a jigsaw or fretsaw and attach to the front of the roof with brads and glue. You can easily vary the pattern of the trim, but the finished width should be around ¾in (18mm) wide.

14 Finally, cut out the 3½in (90mm) wide and 4¼in (108mm) high door shape from a scrap of the ⅜in (9mm) MDF and glue it to the front of the birdhouse.

15 Coat all the remaining sections with the eggshell paint.

This is a large birdhouse, best in a big yard with plenty of trees.

THE DOVECOTE IS

ONE OF THE

MOST TRADITIONAL

AND CLASSIC DESIGNS

FOR A BIRDHOUSE. THIS

OCTAGONAL VERSION HAS SEMI-

CIRCULAR OPENINGS FOR THE BIRDS

WITH EXTERNAL DOWEL PERCHES.

INSIDE THERE ARE THIN PARTITIONS,

DIVIDING THE BIRDHOUSE INTO

MATERIALS

- 4ft square (1220mm²) section of ½in (12mm) thick Exterior Grade plywood
- 2ft (600mm) square section of ¼in (6mm) plywood for internal partitions
- Strips of 1¼ x 1in (30 x 25mm) oak or softwood for edging
- 7ft (2140mm) oak board, approx. 7in (175mm) wide and 1in (25mm) thick
- Softwood strips 1½ x 1in (38 x 25mm) for internal plywood section supports
- 1 x ¼in (25 x 6mm) softwood strip for roof
- 2ft (600mm) of ½in (12.5mm) dowel
- 1½in (38mm) screw
- Brads
- Sandpaper
- Yellow glue
- Wood preservative or gloss paint

TOOLS

- Jigsaw
- Hand saw
- Web clamp
- Hand plane
- Try square
- Tape measure and pencil
- Screwdriver
- Router or rabbet bit
- Electric drill, drill bit
- Hammer
- Paintbrush

FALSE DOVECOTE ////

SEPARATE COMPARTMENTS – SO

EACH ARCHED ENTRANCE LEADS TO

A SEPARATE NESTING AREA. THE

FALSE DOVECOTE IS MADE FROM

EXTERIOR GRADE PLYWOOD WITH

INTERNAL SUPPORTING BATTENS AND

THE ROOF HAS IMITATION SOLID

TONGUE-AND-GROOVE TYPE

CLADDING.

SUITABILITY

- Some birds like to nest in groups and this bijou residence will provide a home for six families. Purple martins, for example, tend to live in colonies and will return year after year to the same aerial apartment complex. Place the birdhouse 15–20ft (4.5–6m) high on a pole in an open area – ideally near open water – and at least 15ft (4.5m) from the nearest overhanging branches or buildings. Purple martins enjoy eating finely crushed egg shells, so scatter a handful on the ground near their house. Before constructing a martin house, find out whether they occur in your area.

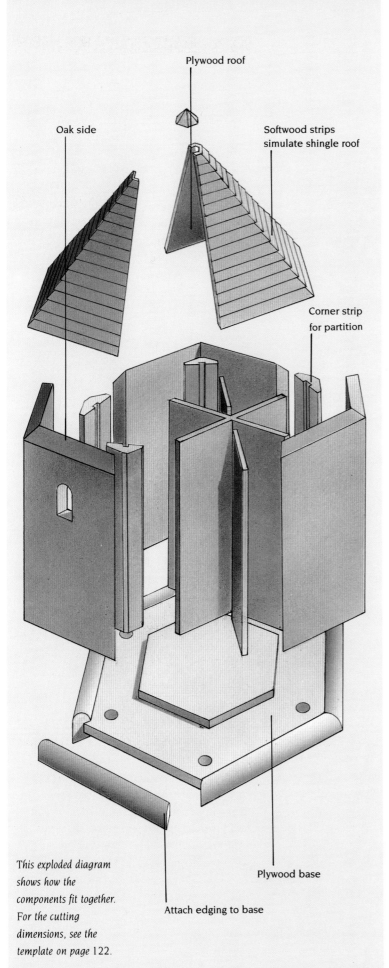

Plywood roof

Oak side

Softwood strips
simulate shingle roof

Corner strip
for partition

Plywood base

Attach edging to base

*This exploded diagram
shows how the
components fit together.
For the cutting
dimensions, see the
template on page 122.*

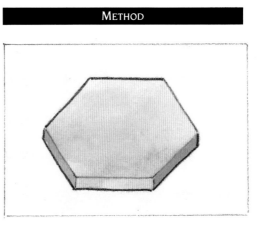

1 Cut the dovecote base from the plywood board following the template shown on page 122.

2 Make a smaller six-sided cut-out, to act as a support for the oak side pieces.

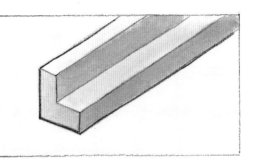

3 Center and align the smaller piece, then screw it on to the base.

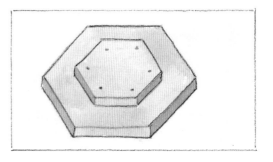

4 Either use ready-made solid wood moldings or form your own rabbet on the strip of 1¼ x 1in (30 x 25mm) softwood. The rabbet should be the depth of the base board.

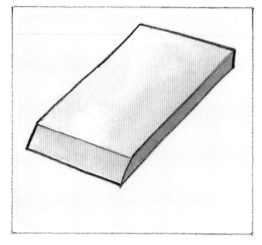

5 Cut the rabbeted strip into pieces longer than each side of the base and miter the ends, trimming until you have an exact fit.

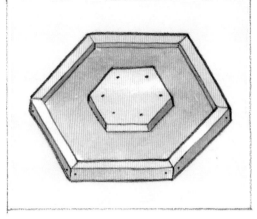

6 Attach the edging to the board with brads and glue, flush with the underside of the base.

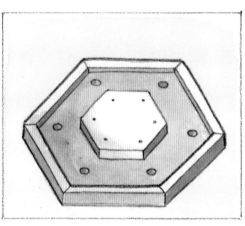

7 Drill drainage holes next to each point of the base, just inside the edging strips. Drill a further six holes nearer the center to allow any water that enters the dovecote to escape.

REMINISCENT OF A BYGONE AGE, THIS DOVECOTE IS TRIANGULAR IN SHAPE.

8 Cut the oak board into 11½in (292mm) lengths for the sides. Plane the top of each side to 45° so that a smooth joint will be formed with the roof sections.

9 Plane the long edges of each oak side piece so that they fit around the smaller six-sided shape.

10 Form an entry hole in each piece of oak, three near the top and three at the bottom. Drill a large 1in (25mm) hole and two smaller holes just above. Then connect the three with a jigsaw.

11 Drill holes at the very bottom of each side so that the sides can be screwed to the small base support at a later stage.

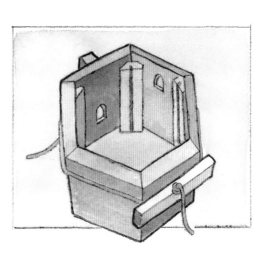

15 Assemble all the strips and side pieces, using glue and screws. Use a web clamp to hold all the pieces firmly until the glue has set.

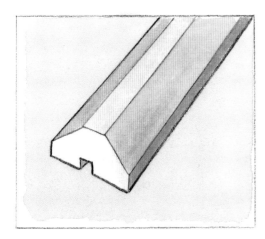

12 Plane two edges of the 1½ x 1in (38 x 25mm) softwood strip and form a ¼in (6mm) rabbet down the center on the other face, to hold the plywood partitions.

13 Cut the finished strip into six pieces, slightly shorter than the oak sides.

14 Take each strip and drill two holes for screws at both the top and the bottom.

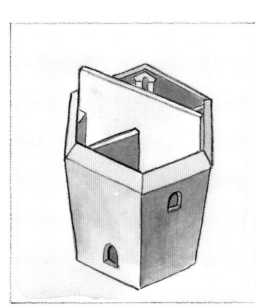

16 Cut out the thinner plywood partitions to fit into the rabbets on the wood strips. In two of the partitions, cut slots halfway up their length in the center. Then slot these two partition pieces together and push them into the dovecote.

OUR FALSE DOVECOTE WAS BASED ON THIS TYPE OF FREE-STANDING BIRDHOUSE WITH TRADITIONAL STYLING.

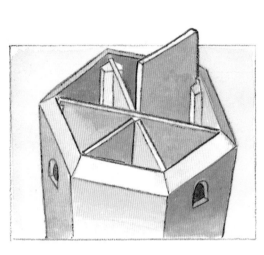

17 The remaining two narrower partition pieces can now be slid into position on each side of the slotted sections, completing the partitioning.

18 Cut out six triangular-shaped roof panels from the ½in (12.5mm) plywood and plane the edges to fit together.

19 Screw and glue each piece to the top of the oak sides, using more glue between the sections.

WALL-MOUNTED BIRDHOUSES, SUCH AS THIS DOVECOTE, CAN BE PARTICULARLY SAFE FROM PREDATORS IF WELL POSITIONED.

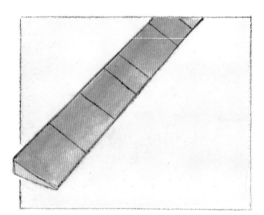

20 Cut the bottom roofing strips to length, mitering the ends so that they match the roof shape formed by the plywood. Decorate with random shallow saw cuts on one side, to simulate a shingle roof.

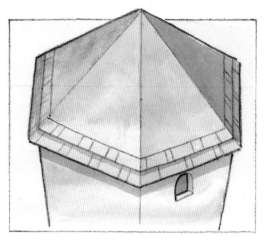

21 Attach the strips to the roof in slightly overlapping rows, cutting each piece so that it follows the line of the roof. Attach with glue and brads. Cut off the apex of the roof with a hand saw.

22 Next, make up a six-sided decorative piece from hardwood and bevel the top edges. Glue this to the top of the roof.

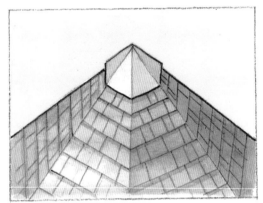

23 Drill ½in (12.5mm) holes below each entrance hole and glue in dowel perches.

24 To form a shelter, jigsaw a bowed shape from scraps of the oak board and glue above the entrance holes.

25 Screw the dovecote to its base and plug the screw holes with solid wood. These should not be glued since you will need to open the dovecote for cleaning.

This dovecote will look most attractive if you paint it with exterior gloss paint. You could, if you prefer, use a clear preservative finish to show off the natural color of the oak. The softwood roof could then be stained to match. Although intended as a nesting box, you could also use it as a feeder. However, this will deter birds from nesting.

MATERIALS

- 20in (500mm) length of 10 x 1in (250 x 25mm) planed pine
- 20in (500mm) length of 1in (25mm) square planed pine
- 10 x 16in (250 x 400mm) piece of ³⁄₁₆in (5mm) thick birch-faced Exterior Grade plywood
- 20in (500mm) length of 4in square (100mm²) planed pine
- 5ft (1.5m) length of ¾ x 6in (18 x 150mm) planed pine
- 3in (75mm) length of ¼in (6mm) diameter hardwood dowel
- 10ft (3m) length of rope (or plated chain)
- 1½in (38mm) brads
- 4 medium-sized plated eyebolts
- Sandpaper
- Piece of light-weight poster board
- Yellow glue
- Exterior Grade clear varnish
- 10 No. 6 x 1¼in (30mm) plated wood screws

TOOLS

- Jigsaw
- Backsaw
- Electric drill (and drill stand if available)
- Set of assorted twist drill bits
- C-clamps
- Pair of compasses
- Coping saw
- Rasp
- Coarse rasp
- Hammer
- Bracing board
- 1½in (38mm) diameter hole saw
- Screwdriver
- Paintbrushes
- Scissors
- Plane

THIS BIBLICAL BIRDHOUSE CAN BE HUNG BY A CHAIN OR ROPE FROM A BRANCH OR A HOOK, AND IT CAN ALSO BE CONVERTED FOR USE AS A FEEDER. MADE OF PINE AND BIRCH-

NOAH'S ARK 〃〃

FACED PLYWOOD, THE DECK EFFECT IS ACHIEVED BY CUTTING SHALLOW GROOVES WITH A BACKSAW. THE BIRDS' ENTRANCE IS IN THE CABIN ON DECK. ALTHOUGH THIS ARK IS TOO SMALL TO HOLD TWO OF EVERY SPECIES ON EARTH, IT WILL MAKE A WONDERFUL HOME FOR A PAIR OF YOUR FEATHERED FRIENDS.

SUITABILITY

- Although this ark is unlikely to be chosen by any doves – they prefer to build a platform-type of nest – it would interest a number of other species. With the 1½in (38mm) hole where it is in this size box, it is suitable for the tree swallow, house wren, and tufted titmouse. It is also possible to use this ark as a feeder instead of a nesting box by placing food on the deck. It is, however, rather unlikely that any birds will take up residence if it is also being used as a restaurant.

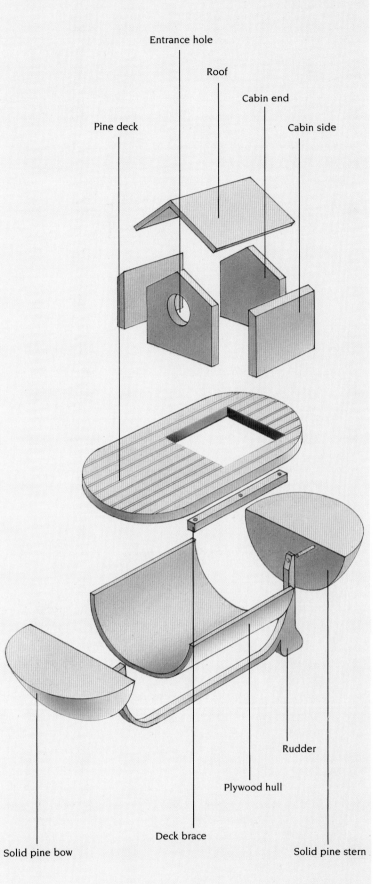

Entrance hole

Roof

Cabin end

Cabin side

Pine deck

Rudder

Plywood hull

Deck brace

Solid pine bow

Solid pine stern

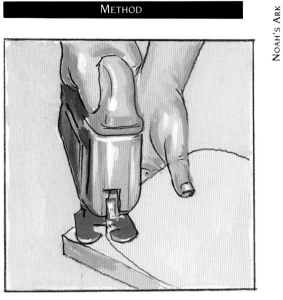

1 To make the deck, lay out two semicircles with a pair of compasses on either end of the piece of 10 x 1in (250 x 25mm) pine so that the distance from end to end is 16in (400mm). Cut along the line with a jigsaw.

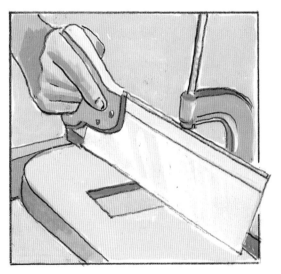

2 Using a scrap piece of wood as a guide (held in place with C-clamps), cut shallow grooves (⅞in (22mm) apart) on the deck with a backsaw.

This exploded diagram shows how the components fit together. For the cutting dimensions, see the template on page 123.

5 Bend over the plywood to form the hull and glue this to the other side of the deck. You may need someone's assistance for this job – to apply the clamps while you bend the plywood.

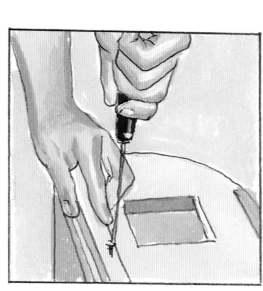

3 From the length of 1in square (25mm²) pine cut two pieces 8½in (215mm) long. Drill three countersunk holes in each ³⁄₁₆in (5mm) and attach them to the underside of the deck, ³⁄₁₆in (5mm) from the edge, with glue and the No. 6 x 1¼in (32mm) screws.

4 Cut a piece of ³⁄₁₆in (5mm) plywood to a width of 8½in (215mm) and a length of 13in (330mm) (note that the plywood will bend more easily one way than the other so think carefully about the way that it is cut). Glue and clamp one edge of the plywood to one side of the deck using a scrap piece of wood to distribute the pressure. Place some newspaper under the scrap wood to prevent it from sticking to the hull. Leave this to set over 24 hours

6 From the length of 4in square (100mm²) pine, cut two pieces 10in (250mm) long; with compasses mark a quadrant on both ends of each piece. Trim them to shape with a plane. Glue and clamp them to the front and back of the hull and leave overnight to set. These will form the bow and stern of the boat.

THIS UNUSUAL BIRDHOUSE HAS BEEN MADE FROM STEAMED PLANKS. STEAMING ALLOWS YOU TO BEND WOOD INTO A CURVED SHAPE, BUT REQUIRES SPECIAL EQUIPMENT.

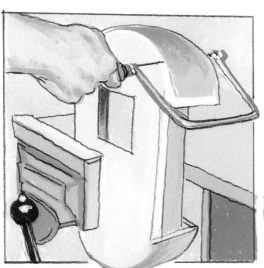

7 Using the profile of the deck as a guide, cut off the excess wood with a coping saw.

9 Lay out the profile of the rudder and bow on a piece of poster board and cut out with a pair of scissors. Using these as templates, lay out the shapes on the 6 x 1⅛in (150 x 28mm) pine. Cut out the profiles using the jigsaw fitted with a fine scrolling blade. Glue and nail the rudder and the bow to the hull.

10 On the remaining 6 x ¾in (150 x 18mm) pine, lay out the sides and roof of the cabin. Cut these with a backsaw and a sawing board.

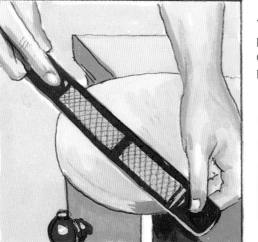

8 Finish the shaping process with a coarse rasp to achieve a quarter sphere shape on either end of the hull. Make a template from a scrap piece of plywood which you can "offer up" to the nose as a shape tester. Cut away the nose until it is level with the plywood. Be careful not to cut into the plywood with the rasp. Remove rasp marks with medium grade sandpaper.

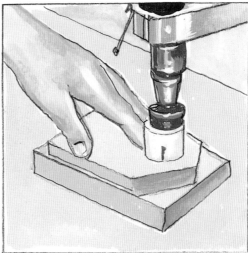

11 Using an electric drill and a hole saw, make a 1½in (38mm) entry hole for the birds in one of the cabin ends. A drill stand is not essential but it helps. Clean the internal edge of the hole with sandpaper.

THIS TRADITIONAL NEST BOX IS JUST LIKE THE HOUSE THAT SITS ON NOAH'S ARK ALTHOUGH THE EXTRA WOOD DETAILING ON THE ROOF AND A COAT OF PAINT HAVE TRANSFORMED IT.

12 Assemble the cabin with glue and brads and, when it is dry, trim any uneven surfaces with a plane.

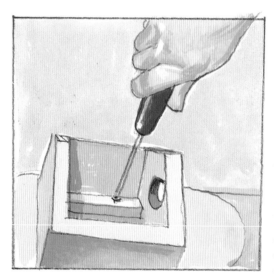

13 Cut two lengths of wood scraps to a length of 4⅜in (110mm). Drill two ⁄₁₆in (5mm) countersunk holes in each and glue them to the inside base of the cabin. When the glue has set, attach the cabin to the deck with four No. 6 x 1¼in (32mm) screws.

14 Using 1½in (38mm) brads and glue, attach the roof to the cabin.

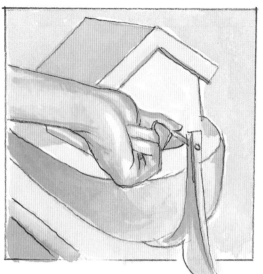

15 Glue the tiller, made from ¼in (6mm) dowel, into the pre-drilled hole on the rudder.

16 Sand off any remaining pencil or saw marks with medium grade grit sandpaper prior to varnishing. When the varnish has dried, sand with fine grade grit sandpaper, dust and apply another coat of varnish. Repeat this process for a third application of varnish.

17 Drill ⅛in (3mm) pilot holes on the deck and screw in plated eye bolts. Attach rope or chain to the eyebolts so that you can suspend the birdhouse.

You may not be Noah, but with this birdhouse you can provide a family of birds with shelter from the weather.

FOR AN URBAN YARD OR A

ROOF TERRACE, HERE IS A

THOROUGHLY MODERN, CITY

BIRDFEEDER. THERE ARE TWO SIDE

TOWERS THAT CAN BE USED FOR

DIFFERENT SORTS OF FOOD AND

EACH TOWER HAS A HINGED,

SLOPING TOP SO IT CAN BE REFILLED

EASILY. WOODEN DOWELS,

MATERIALS
● 30in (750mm) length of 4in square (100mm²) softwood
● 40 x 24in (1000 x 600mm) piece of ¼in (6mm) Exterior Grade MDF
● 24 x 16in (600 x 400mm) piece of ¾in (18mm) Exterior Grade MDF
● Brads
● Staples
● Two small yogurt cups
● Length of bicycle tire inner tube
● Yellow glue
● Two No. 4 x ⅜in (9mm) plated roundhead screws
● Galvanized wire mesh
● Exterior Grade paint
● Sandpaper

TOOLS
● Handsaw
● Plane
● Backsaw
● Hammer
● Sliding bevel or miter square
● Electric drill
● ¾in (18mm) spade bit
● ¾in (18mm) chisel
● Mallet
● Metal snips
● Heavy duty stapler
● Scissors
● Awl
● ⅛in (3mm) twist drill bit
● Screwdriver
● Paintbrushes

SKYSCRAPER ////

DISTINGUISHED AS FLAGPOLES, GIVE

THE BIRDS A PERCHING PLACE

DURING FEEDING. THE TWO SMALLER

TOWERS HAVE POTS IN WHICH IVY

CAN BE PLANTED, WHILE THE

TALLEST TOWER HAS A PAINTED TOP

TO GIVE THE EFFECT OF A COPPER

ROOF, AND THIS MOTIF IS REPEATED

AS A TRIANGLE OVER THE FRONT

ENTRANCE.

SUITABILITY
● This elaborate feeder has two flaps that open so that the food store can be refilled. Try experimenting with different food in each tower. You will soon get to know the species that regularly use your feeder and can give them particular treats. Use a small mesh on one side for thistle (niger) seed for American goldfinches, and pine siskins. A larger mesh on the other tower could hold sunflower seeds or hearts for purple finches, titmice, chickadees, and nuthatches. Jays cannot resist peanuts, so you may want to reserve a tower as their special feeder.

This exploded diagram
shows how the
components fit together.
For the cutting
dimensions, see the
template on page 124.

Lid for feed store

Windows painted on

Inner pyramid of softwood

Outer covering of MDF

Wire mesh for feeder

Side of grain store

Bottom of grain store

Scrap of wood
used to make door

Front of grain store

Dowel perches

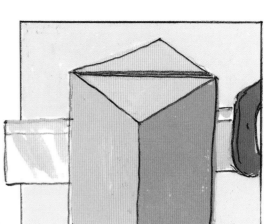

1 Using a handsaw, cut the softwood
diagonally through its length and plane off
any saw marks.

2 From the resultant triangular material, lay
out and cut to a length of 24in (600mm) for
the lower inner structure.

3 On the ¼in (6mm) MDF lay out and cut
with a jigsaw one piece 4¾ x 24in
(120 x 600mm) and one piece 4½ x 24in
(114 x 600mm). Trim to the line with a plane
and then nail and glue these two pieces to
the inner structure.

4 On the remaining piece of softwood, lay
out half a pyramid, cut with a backsaw and
plane off any saw marks; then glue this to the
top of the inner structure.

5 From the piece of ¾in (18mm) MDF mark and cut two lengths with a jigsaw and accurately plane to a width of 4¼in (108mm). Cut one piece to a length of 13in (330mm) and the other 17in (430mm). With a plane, bevel one end of both pieces to an angle of 45°, checking for accuracy with a sliding bevel or a miter square. Cut and accurately trim another two pieces of ¾in (18mm) MDF to 4¼ x 2¼in (108 x 56mm). Glue and nail one to the end of the 13in (330mm) length of ¾in (18mm) MDF and the other 4in (100mm) up from the end of the other. These will form the rear structure and bottoms of the grain store.

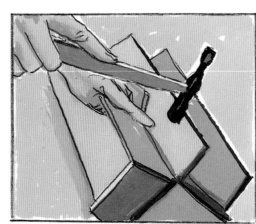

6 Glue and nail the grain store structure to the main part of the bird feeder.

7 Lay out and cut the sides, fronts, and lids of the grain store from the ¼in (6mm) MDF; cut 45° angles on the side pieces.

8 Glue and nail these to the rear structure and bottoms of the grain stores.

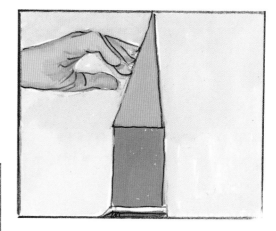

9 From the remaining ¼in (6mm) MDF, cut two isosceles triangles with a base length of 4¾in (120mm) and other two sides of 9¾in (250mm). Trim the bases of the triangles at an angle so that they fit accurately on the top of the skyscraper. When fitting is completed, glue and nail these to the top to form the roof of the feeder.

12 With the plane, bevel the top ends of the grain store fronts to correspond with the 45° angle of the sides.

10 On the fronts of the feeders, lay out three rectangles with a craft knife. With an electric drill fitted with an ¾in (18mm) spade bit, drill out as much of the material as possible inside each rectangle.

13 Cut the wire mesh with wire cutters and staple this to the inside of the grain store fronts.

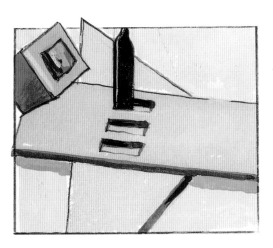

11 Use a chisel and mallet to cut out the remainder of the MDF to knife line, so that the rectangles are accurate.

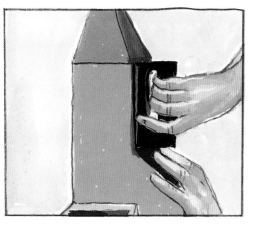

14 Glue and nail the grain store fronts in position.

A HORIZONTAL RATHER THAN VERTICAL EXAMPLE OF A COLONY BIRDHOUSE, THAT WOULD MAKE AN ATTRACTIVE FEATURE ATTACHED TO A WALL.

15 Sand the feeder with medium grit sandpaper, removing any irregularities in the jointing and apply a coat of primer paint. When the primer has dried, sand with fine grade grit sandpaper and apply undercoat paint. Complete painting with a finishing color. Highlight windows and roofs with a darker, contrasting color.

16 Cut lengths of bike tire inner tube and staple it to the edges of the grain store lids/roofs.

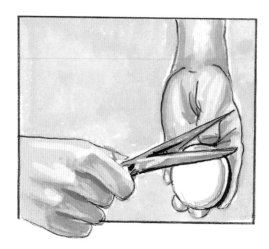

18 With a pair of scissors, cut two yogurt cups at an angle of 45°, drill ⅛in (3mm) holes in the center of the base and then paint.

17 In turn, staple the lids into position on the tops of the grain store to make a hinge.

19 Mark the centers of the grain store lids/roofs and make indentations with an awl; screw two yogurt cups in position. Alternatively, cut a round hole in each roof and fit the pots in place.

This high-rise feeder is particularly useful for city-dwellers who have little space for storage, since the grain store will hold enough seed for several weeks, and the feeding cups can be filled very easily.

You can enlarge the templates on a photocopier–for example, to make each dimension twice as large, you would set the copier for 200 percent. Alternatively just use a pencil and rule to lay out the pieces on your wood or board.

SILENT GARDENER (SEE P.38)

MONKEY NUTS (SEE P.31)

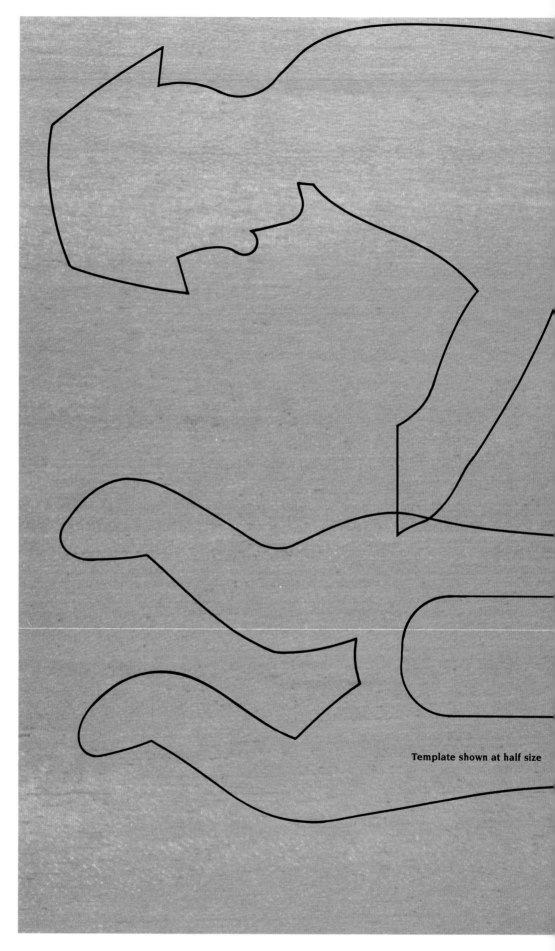

Template shown at half size

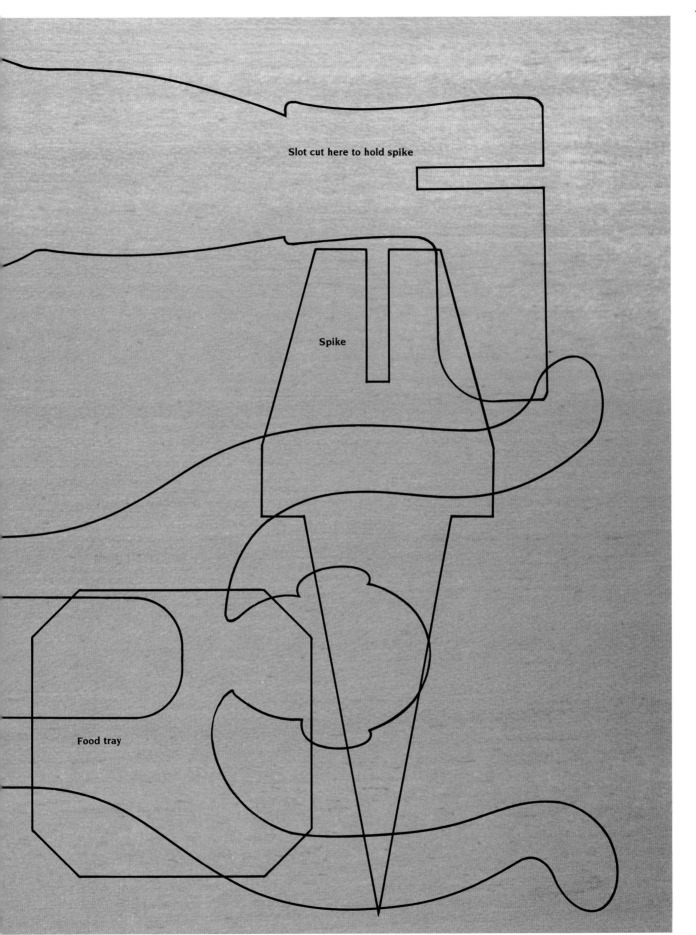

Slot cut here to hold spike

Spike

Food tray

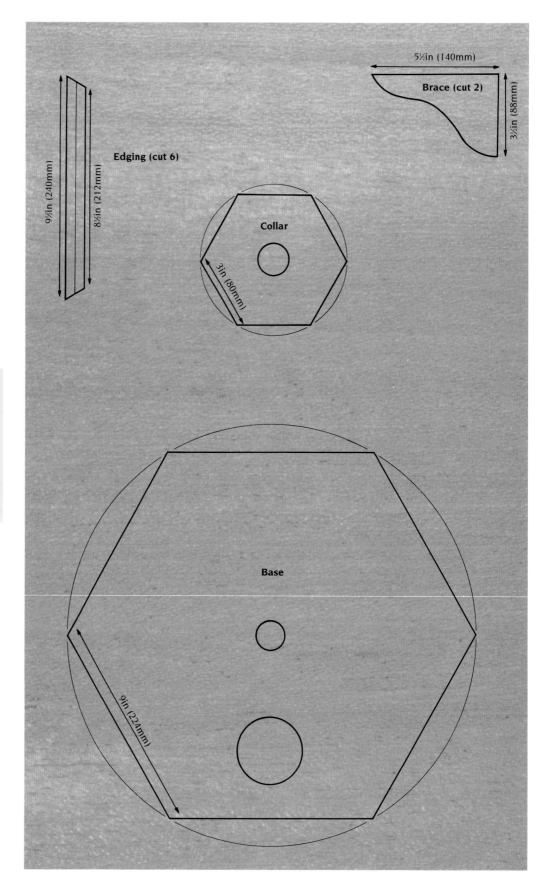

Brace (cut 2)

5½in (140mm)

3½in (88mm)

Edging (cut 6)

9½in (240mm)

8⅓in (212mm)

Collar

3in (80mm)

Base

9in (224mm)

GARDENER'S FRIEND
(SEE P.24)

End panel (cut 2, 1 with entrance hole)

3in (80mm)

Entrance hole

1in (25mm) diameter

6in (150mm)

6in (150mm)

Side panel (cut 2)

6in (150mm)

12in (300mm)

Roof (cut 2)

3¼in (80mm)

12in (300mm)

Base

6in (150mm)

12in (300mm)

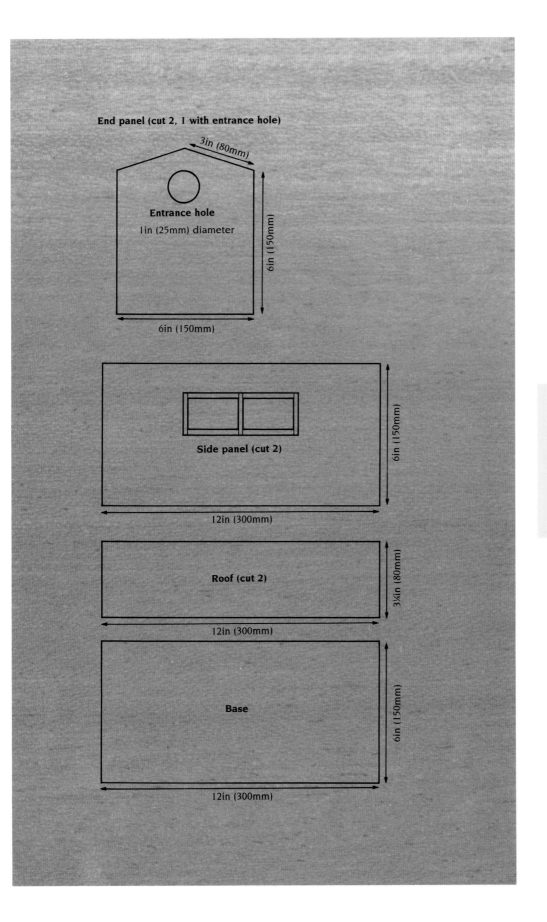

MINI SHED (SEE P.34)

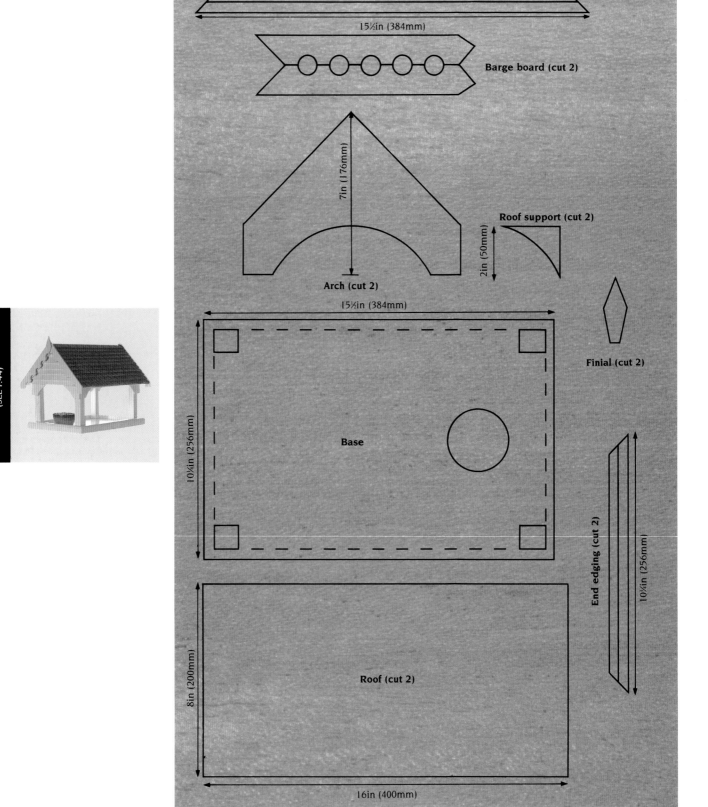

Side edging (cut 2)

15½in (384mm)

Barge board (cut 2)

7in (176mm)

Roof support (cut 2)

2in (50mm)

Arch (cut 2)

Finial (cut 2)

15½in (384mm)

Base

10¼in (256mm)

End edging (cut 2)

10¼in (256mm)

Roof (cut 2)

8in (200mm)

16in (400mm)

8¾in (220mm)

Roof (cut 2)

8in (200mm)

End panel (cut 2, 1 with entrance hole)

12⅝in (320mm)

Side panel (cut 2)

7in (175mm)

9in (225mm)

Entrance hole

1¼in (30mm) diameter

7in (175mm)

8in (200mm)

3⅜in (85mm)

Door

Window (cut 4)

1¾in (45mm)

2in (50mm)

1¾in (45mm)

Base

9in (225mm)

2⅞in (72mm)

1¾in (45mm)

8in (200mm)

Dormer window (cut 2)

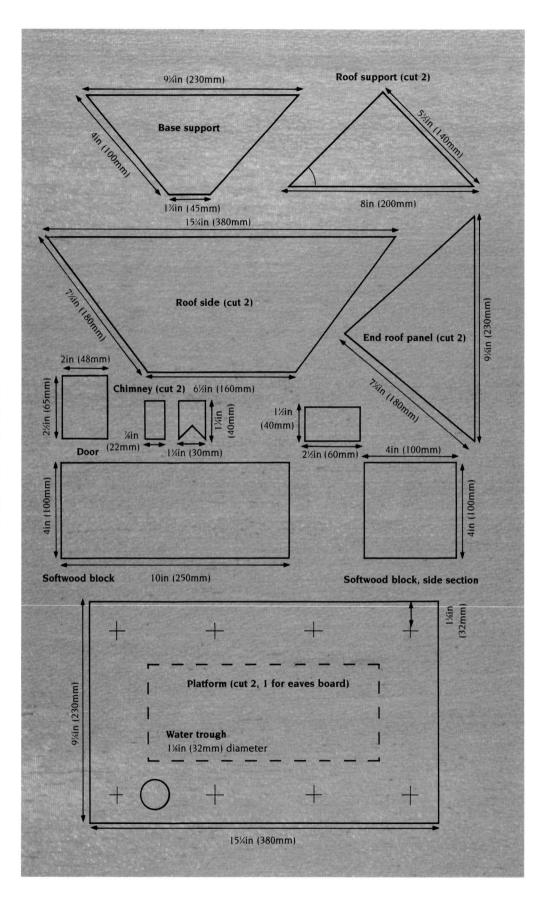

9¼in (230mm)

Roof support (cut 2)

Base support

5½in (140mm)

4in (100mm)

1¾in (45mm)

8in (200mm)

15¼in (380mm)

7¼in (180mm)

Roof side (cut 2)

9¼in (230mm)

End roof panel (cut 2)

7¼in (180mm)

2in (48mm)

2⅝in (65mm)

Chimney (cut 2)   6½in (160mm)

1½in (40mm)

1½in (40mm)

⅞in (22mm)

1¼in (30mm)

Door

1½in (40mm)

4in (100mm)

4in (100mm)

2½in (60mm)

4in (100mm)

Softwood block   10in (250mm)

Softwood block, side section

1¼in (32mm)

9¼in (230mm)

Platform (cut 2, 1 for eaves board)

Water trough
1¼in (32mm) diameter

15¼in (380mm)

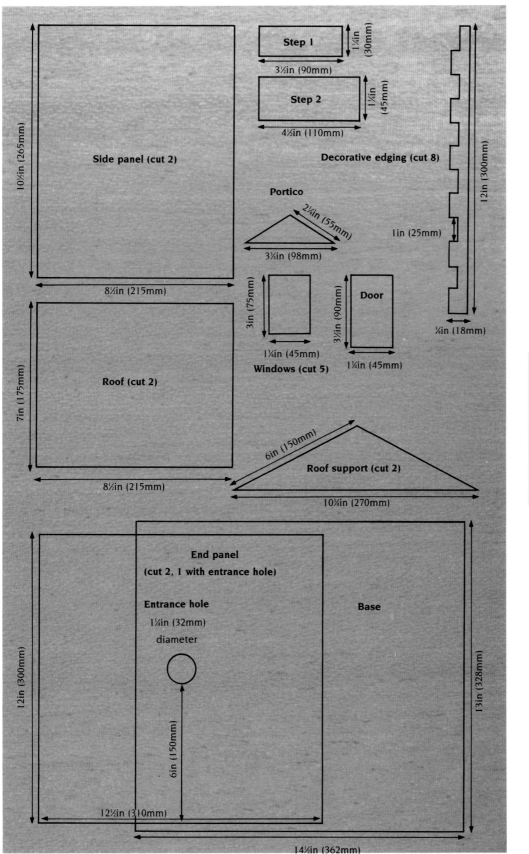

Step 1

1¼in (30mm)

3½in (90mm)

Step 2

1¾in (45mm)

4⅓in (110mm)

Decorative edging (cut 8)

Side panel (cut 2)

10½in (265mm)

8½in (215mm)

12in (300mm)

1in (25mm)

Portico

2¼in (55mm)

3⅞in (98mm)

3in (75mm)

1¾in (45mm)

Door

3½in (90mm)

1¾in (45mm)

Windows (cut 5)

¾in (18mm)

Roof (cut 2)

7in (175mm)

8½in (215mm)

6in (150mm)

Roof support (cut 2)

10¾in (270mm)

End panel
(cut 2, 1 with entrance hole)

Entrance hole

1¼in (32mm)
diameter

Base

12in (300mm)

6in (150mm)

13in (328mm)

12½in (310mm)

14⅛in (362mm)

COUNTRY HOUSE
(SEE P.56)

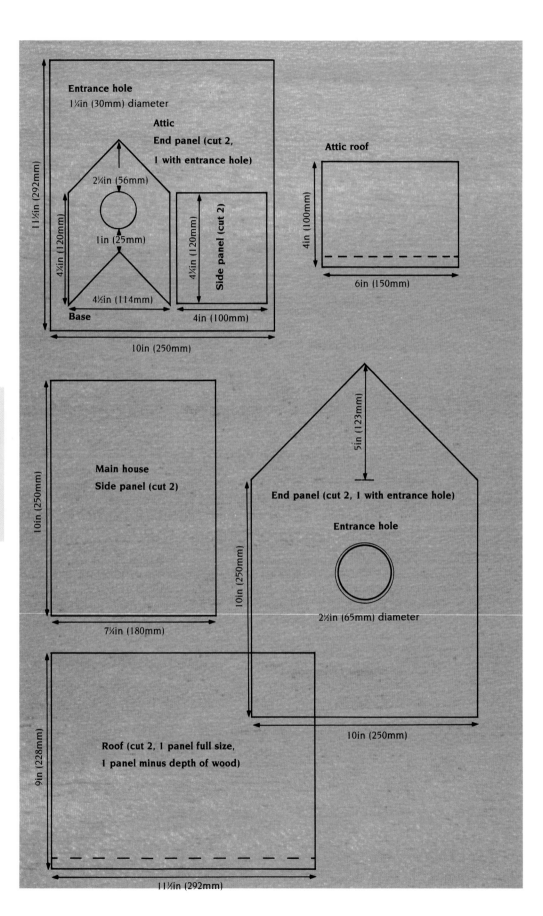

Entrance hole

1¼in (30mm) diameter

Attic

**End panel (cut 2,
1 with entrance hole)**

2¼in (56mm)

1in (25mm)

4¾in (120mm)

4½in (114mm)

Base

11½in (292mm)

10in (250mm)

Side panel (cut 2)

4¾in (120mm)

4in (100mm)

Attic roof

4in (100mm)

6in (150mm)

**Main house
Side panel (cut 2)**

10in (250mm)

7¼in (180mm)

5in (123mm)

End panel (cut 2, 1 with entrance hole)

Entrance hole

2½in (65mm) diameter

10in (250mm)

10in (250mm)

9in (228mm)

**Roof (cut 2, 1 panel full size,
1 panel minus depth of wood)**

11½in (292mm)

Cross

2in (50mm)

1½in (38mm)

3in (75mm)

1½in (38mm)

Side window (cut 3)

6in (160mm)

8in (210mm)

3in (75mm)

4in (100mm)

Bell

¾in (20mm)

7½in (190mm)

2in (50mm)

End panel (cut 2, 1 with space for bell)

Door

End window (cut 2)

2in (50mm) square

1in (30mm)

3in (75mm)

Dowel holes

6in (160mm)

Slot opening

1½in (38mm)

11in (280mm)

Side panel (cut 2, 1 with slot entrance)

13¾in (350mm)

7½in (190mm)

Roof/floor (cut 2)

13¾in (350mm)

MISSION CHURCH
(SEE P.64)

TUDOR COTTAGE (SEE P.70)

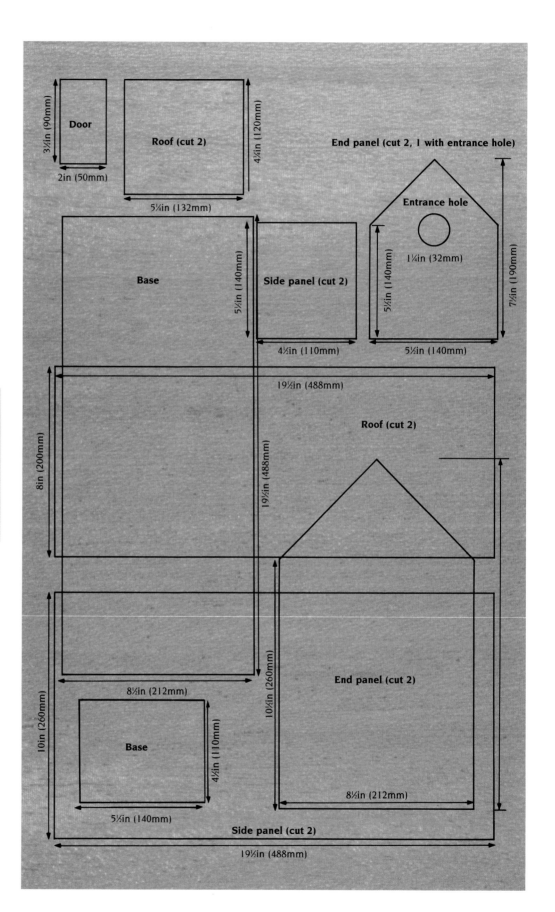

Door

3½in (90mm)

2in (50mm)

Roof (cut 2)

4¾in (120mm)

5¼in (132mm)

End panel (cut 2, 1 with entrance hole)

Entrance hole

1¼in (32mm)

5½in (140mm)

7½in (190mm)

5½in (140mm)

Base

5½in (140mm)

Side panel (cut 2)

4⅓in (110mm)

19¼in (488mm)

Roof (cut 2)

8in (200mm)

19¼in (488mm)

End panel (cut 2)

10¼in (260mm)

8¼in (212mm)

10in (260mm)

Base

4⅓in (110mm)

5½in (140mm)

8¼in (212mm)

Side panel (cut 2)

19¼in (488mm)

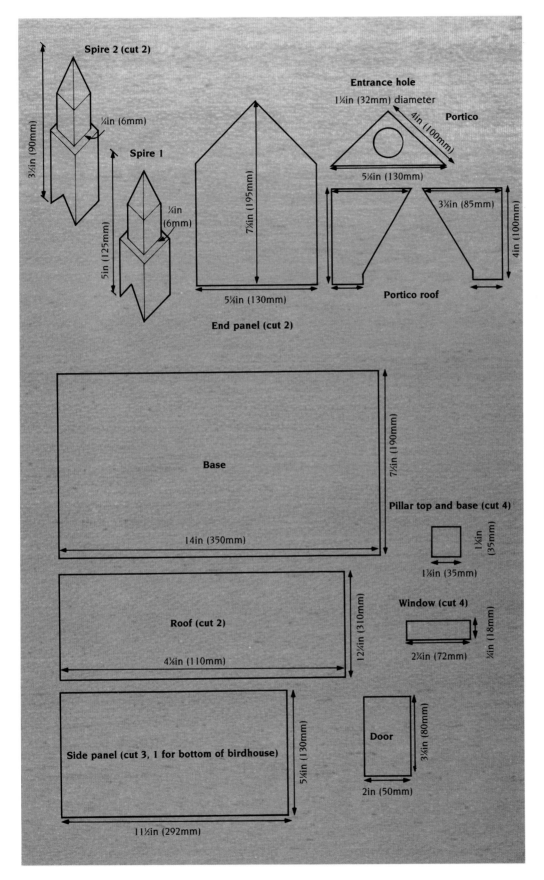

Spire 2 (cut 2)

3½in (90mm)

¼in (6mm)

Spire 1

5in (125mm)

¼in (6mm)

Entrance hole

1¼in (32mm) diameter

Portico

4in (100mm)

5⅛in (130mm)

3⅜in (85mm)

4in (100mm)

Portico roof

7⅝in (195mm)

5⅛in (130mm)

End panel (cut 2)

Base

7½in (190mm)

14in (350mm)

Pillar top and base (cut 4)

1⅜in (35mm)

1⅜in (35mm)

Window (cut 4)

¾in (18mm)

2¾in (72mm)

Roof (cut 2)

12¼in (310mm)

4⅜in (110mm)

Side panel (cut 3, 1 for bottom of birdhouse)

5⅛in (130mm)

11½in (292mm)

Door

3⅛in (80mm)

2in (50mm)

NEOCLASSICAL NESTER
(SEE P.74)

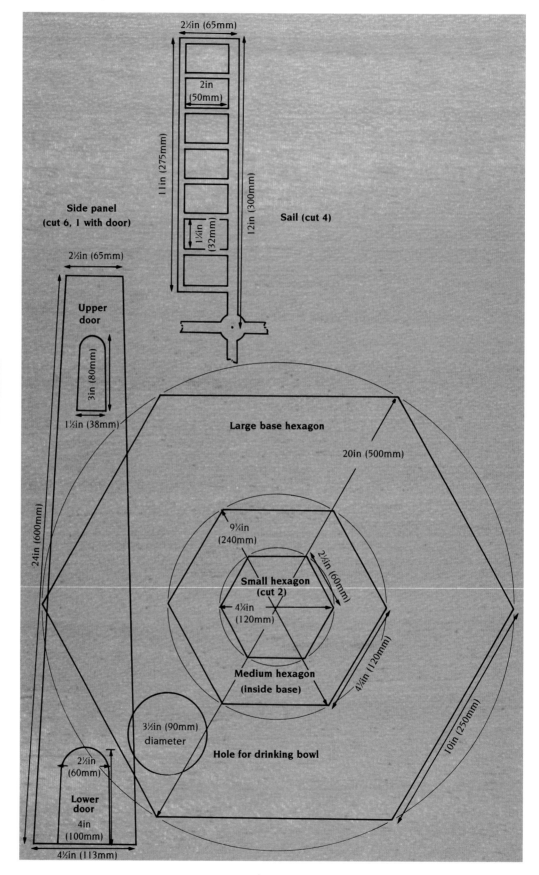

2½in (65mm)

2in (50mm)

11in (275mm)

1¼in (32mm)

12in (300mm)

Sail (cut 4)

**Side panel
(cut 6, 1 with door)**

2½in (65mm)

Upper door

3in (80mm)

1½in (38mm)

Large base hexagon

20in (500mm)

9¾in (240mm)

2¼in (60mm)

**Small hexagon
(cut 2)**

4¾in (120mm)

24in (600mm)

**Medium hexagon
(inside base)**

4¾in (120mm)

4¾in (120mm)

3½in (90mm) diameter

Hole for drinking bowl

10in (250mm)

2¼in (60mm)

Lower door

4in (100mm)

4½in (113mm)

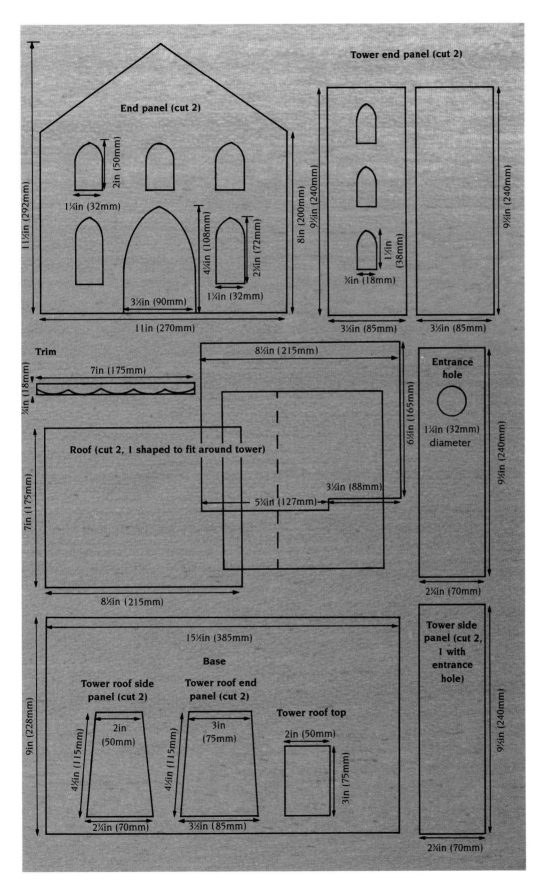

End panel (cut 2)

11½in (292mm)

2in (50mm)

1¼in (32mm)

8in (200mm)

4¼in (108mm)

2¾in (72mm)

3½in (90mm)

1¼in (32mm)

11in (270mm)

Tower end panel (cut 2)

9½in (240mm)

1½in (38mm)

¾in (18mm)

3½in (85mm)

9½in (240mm)

3½in (85mm)

Trim

7in (175mm)

¾in (18mm)

8½in (215mm)

Roof (cut 2, 1 shaped to fit around tower)

7in (175mm)

6½in (165mm)

3½in (88mm)

5¼in (127mm)

8½in (215mm)

Entrance hole

1¼in (32mm) diameter

9½in (240mm)

2¾in (70mm)

15½in (385mm)

Base

9in (228mm)

Tower roof side panel (cut 2)

2in (50mm)

4½in (115mm)

2¾in (70mm)

Tower roof end panel (cut 2)

3in (75mm)

4½in (115mm)

3½in (85mm)

Tower roof top

2in (50mm)

3in (75mm)

Tower side panel (cut 2, 1 with entrance hole)

9½in (240mm)

2¾in (70mm)

GOTHIC MANSION
(SEE P.84)

122

FALSE DOVECOTE
(SEE P.90)

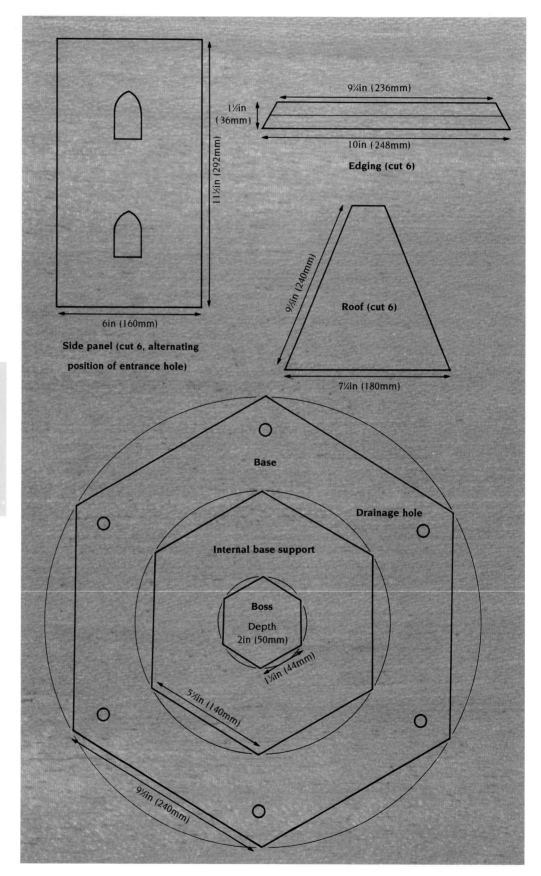

1½in (36mm)

9¼in (236mm)

10in (248mm)

Edging (cut 6)

11½in (292mm)

6in (160mm)

Side panel (cut 6, alternating position of entrance hole)

9½in (240mm)

Roof (cut 6)

7¼in (180mm)

Base

Drainage hole

Internal base support

Boss
Depth
2in (50mm)

1¾in (44mm)

5½in (140mm)

9½in (240mm)

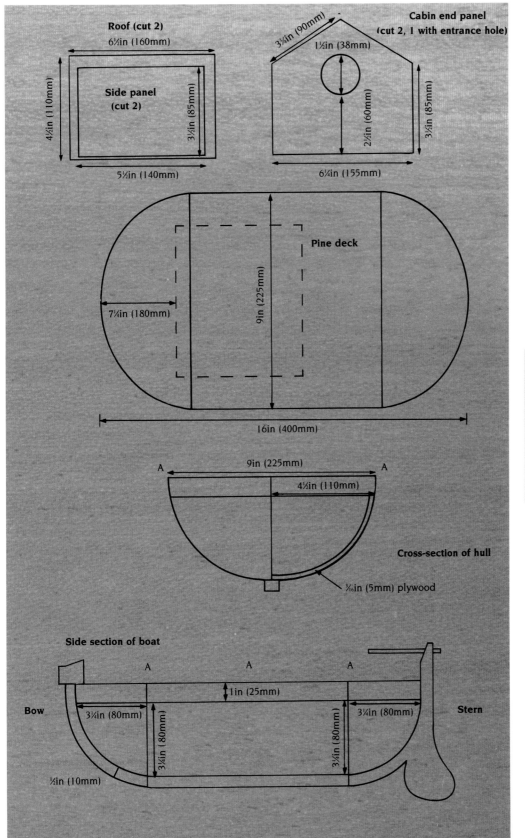

Roof (cut 2)

6½in (160mm)

4½in (110mm)

Side panel (cut 2)

3½in (85mm)

5½in (140mm)

Cabin end panel (cut 2, 1 with entrance hole)

3⅝in (90mm)

1½in (38mm)

2½in (60mm)

3½in (85mm)

6¼in (155mm)

Pine deck

7¼in (180mm)

9in (225mm)

16in (400mm)

A 9in (225mm) A

4½in (110mm)

Cross-section of hull

3⁄16in (5mm) plywood

Side section of boat

A   A   A

1in (25mm)

Bow

3¼in (80mm)

3¼in (80mm)

½in (10mm)

3¼in (80mm)

3¼in (80mm)

Stern

NOAH'S ARK
(SEE P.96)

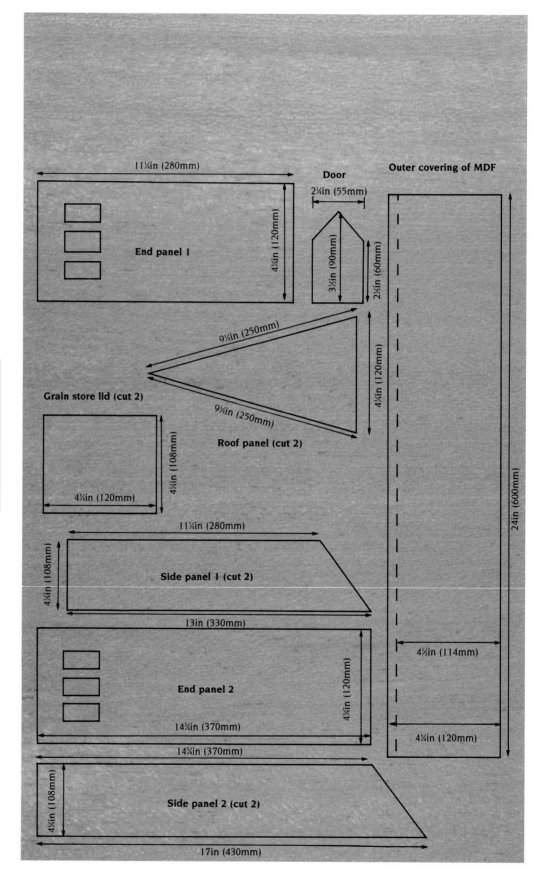

11¼in (280mm)

4¾in (120mm)

End panel 1

Door

2⅛in (55mm)

3½in (90mm)

2⅜in (60mm)

Outer covering of MDF

9⅞in (250mm)

9⅞in (250mm)

4¾in (120mm)

Roof panel (cut 2)

24in (600mm)

Grain store lid (cut 2)

4¼in (108mm)

4¾in (120mm)

4½in (114mm)

11¼in (280mm)

4¼in (108mm)

Side panel 1 (cut 2)

13in (330mm)

4¾in (120mm)

End panel 2

14¾in (370mm)

4¾in (120mm)

14¾in (370mm)

4¼in (108mm)

Side panel 2 (cut 2)

17in (430mm)

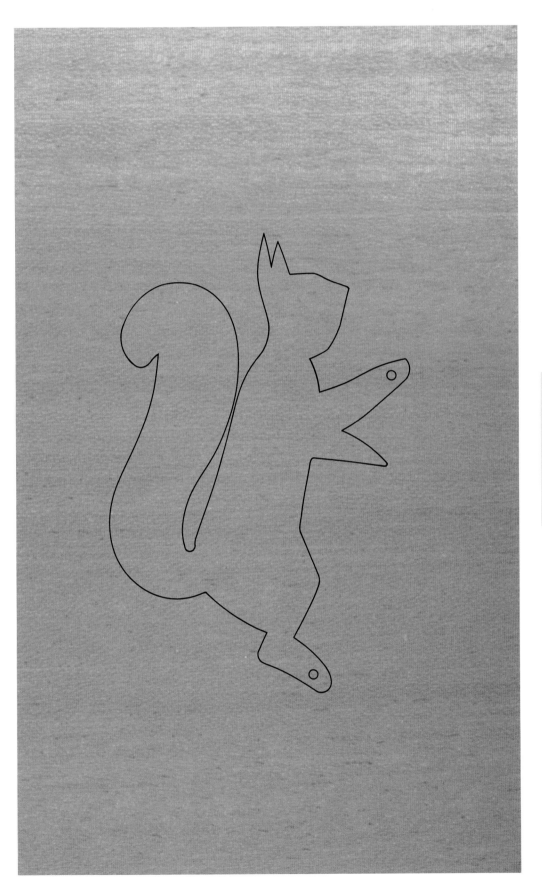

SQUIRREL NUTKIN
(SEE P.41)

INDEX

Numbers in **bold** refer to illustration captions.
Lists of tools and materials at the beginning of
each chapter are not included in the index.

ACKNOWLEDGMENTS

Quarto would like to thank the following for permission to reproduce
photographs in this book:
Ace Photo Agency 10*l* (Margot Melmore), 46 (Erik Pelham);
Heather Angel/Biofotos 10*br*; Daybreak Imagery 6 (Susan Day), 7*a*, 29, 98
(Richard Day); Jesse Hickman 13*al*; Andrew Lawson 13*ar*;
Clifton Monteith 9*b*, 22, 100; Jackie Newey 9*a*, 12, 72, 92; PhotoNats 7*c*
(Deborah M. Clowell), 8 (Priscilla Connell), 101 (Carl Hanninen);
Randy Sewell 13*b*, 50, 54, 82, 99; Harry Smith Collection 76, 93;
Nancy Thomas Studio Gallery 36, 39, 58, 62, 66, 102;
Traditional Garden Supply Ltd 67, 94; Juliette Wade 68, 87;
Wildlife Matters 7*b*, 10*ar*, 11*a* & *b*.
KEY: *a* above, *b* below, *c* center, *l* left, *r* right
All other photographs are the copyright of Quarto Publishing plc.

Quarto would like to thank the following craftsmen who contributed
projects to the book:
FRANK DELICATA, ERIC KENDALL, and BOB PIPER